MAGDALENA

A PROSTITUTE'S LIFE IN COSTA RICA

Thomas Ray O'Brien

Subscribe to my Free Email List for Updates and New Stories

http://www.lovecostaricastyle.com/

Contents

AUTHOR'S NOTE

The following is work of fiction. The inspiration comes from interviews and conversations with numerous prostitutes as well as some of their clients, family members and friends.

Magdalena's Childhood – (1966 - 1974)

I was born in July, 1966. The earliest I can remember was from when I was five or six years old. I lived with my grandmother in Moravia, near San José *[the capital]*. I barely knew my mother at that time. She would visit once in a while and we called her "Mama" but it was just the name we called her. Just what a mother was, we didn't know. Our grandmother was the one who took care of us. "Mama" was only a person we saw once in a while. There were three of us living with my grandmother then. There was me, my sister Yorleny, two years younger than I am, and my brother Rodrigo who was one year younger. We all slept on the dirt floor of my grandmother's house on a plastic sheet with a regular sheet on top and a cover over us.

When I was around six or seven my grandmother died and my mother came and took us from Moravia to a bad neighborhood in Desamparados, south of San José. All I remember of my grandmother's death was her casket. When we moved to our new "home" we lived in a "precario" or "ranchita." *[A shanty/lean-to shack]* with a dirt floor and without electricity, running water or a bathroom. We didn't have any kind of stove or anything like that to cook with. We cooked over an open fire. When we had the money to buy charcoal, we'd cook with charcoal; otherwise my mother would send us out to gather pieces of wood. We would put a piece of tin, like off a tin roof, on top of an old table and put some rocks together, then build a fire between the rocks. Then we would put a pot on top of the rocks and cook the rice and beans. When we were lucky we would have some onions or an egg.

I remember the first time my mother left us alone to go somewhere while the beans were cooking. She left me in to stir the beans but I told my sister Yorleny that SHE had to do it. She argued with me saying I was older and she was too young. I grabbed her by the hair and told her she HAD to do it, and she gave in. It was only about five minutes later that she was stirring the beans. But because she was so small, she had to stand on a little stool to reach them. Well, the pot wasn't all that stable on the rocks, and it tipped over and spilled on her, scalding her chest and stomach, leaving blisters. A neighbor heard Yorleny screaming and took her to the hospital. They treated her, put white cream all over her, and we went back to the ranchita. My mother finally came back late that night and she was angry with us for ruining the beans and angry with me for putting Yorleny in charge. Maybe she was also angry with me for letting Yorleny get hurt, I don't remember that part.

It was after we moved from Moravia that I found out I had an older sister, Patricia (Pati). Pati didn't live with us, but with her godmother, maybe two hours away. But she would sometimes stay with us for one reason or another. We had got a very simple bed by then, just some wood with a thin cover on the bottom and a thin cover on top. I remember sometimes I would put some shirts or whatever I had below the bottom cover to act like a sort of mattress.

My mother washed clothes for other people to earn a little money. It was enough to buy a little something to eat but she spent most of it on guaro [the local Costa Rican liquor, made from sugar cane, something between rum and vodka]. She was an alcoholic then and still is. When she would go out drinking, sometimes she would take us children along. I always liked to dance. I remember one time there was a man there who looked like my grandfather and he asked my mother if he could dance with me. She said yes and so I would dance with him and sometimes he gave me a little money and I bought some candy for myself and to share with my brother and sisters. That was one way we appeased our hunger a little and weren't left alone.

Often I would be left to take care of Rodrigo and Yorleny. Most of the time Pati wasn't around and it was up to me alone to take care of them. This happened a lot because my mother was always in the cantinas, drinking, dancing and such.

We children went hungry a lot of the time. I remember going from house to house, asking for something to eat and sometimes the people would give me a little bread, or something like that. Other times I went to the "mercado" *[farmers open air market]* and I would scavenge for produce that had gone bad and the farmers had thrown away. I remember Pati asking for bones from the butcher shops. That was how we made soup for everybody. We were all so hungry that we all thought the soup was totally delicious! Somehow or other we survived that way until I was about eight or nine.

I don't know why, but I was very young when I began to have sexual feelings. I can't say exactly when it started, but it was long before puberty. I remember that when I would play hide and seek with other children I would hide with other kids so they would sometimes touch my genitals. By the time I was seven or eight, I was masturbating whenever I had the chance. The house was crowded and I didn't get the chance more than once or twice a week, I would say. But when I did masturbate I would bring myself to orgasm. I would masturbate with pillows or with the bed posts. I was always thinking about sexual things. I think it is probably just something I was born with.

My sisters and I all slept in the same bed. Although Pati didn't live with us, she would sometimes spend the night and would sleep with me and Yorleny. I remember once when I must have been around nine years old and Pati was staying with us. We were in bed when I felt Pati's leg move and brush up against my vagina. I thought that she wanted me to touch her too, and I started to touch her vagina. When I did this, she woke up, very afraid, and asked me what I was doing and I got very afraid and I started to cry. I didn't understand then why she hadn't let me continue. I didn't realize it wasn't just something normal to do.

1977 Juan

It was around 1974 when my mother brought a man home from one of the cantinas to live with us. His name was Juan and he was from Nicaragua originally, but he had to leave because he had killed the entire family of the man who had killed his brother. He was running away from the law there.

Juan was as much of an alcoholic then as my mother. Juan worked as a shoemaker. He had a small business with some other men working for him. He would probably have done alright but his drinking was always a problem. He would do well for a while then lose his shop because he was drinking too much. Drinking came before his business. Sometimes he did alright and sometimes he didn't.

I can't say why they got together or stayed together, but they are still together after all these years. They used to argue all the time and even hit each other. They still do, although Juan has given up drinking. But they're still together, amazing as that is.

Rodrigo, Yorleny and I would watch them drinking and fighting just about every night. My mother would usually pass out before Juan, and he would climb on top of her and have sex with her right in front of us.

Besides hitting my mother, Juan would hit us children too, sometimes. But more than hitting us he liked to fondle us, touch us... the girls anyway... in nasty ways. My mother wasn't so drunk or stupid that she didn't know, but she let it go on. I've been in a lot of relationships myself and I NEVER let anybody touch my children.

Yorleny and I lived in fear of Juan, more for his molesting us than hitting us. When Yorleny and I would sleep, there would be times when we would wake up because he was groping us. I was already sexual by then, but I didn't want anything to do with Juan. He was so much older, and drunk so often, and even violent with us. And he was my mother's boyfriend on top of all that. She was and still is very jealous, and I was afraid she would blame ME for anything that happened.

So when my mother was passed out or sleeping, my sister and brother and I had to hide ourselves and put the clothes dresser up against the door of our room because if we didn't, Juan would come in and try to molest Yorleny and me. We lived in fear that he would rape us and there was nothing we could do about it, at least nothing we knew of. Hunger and fear of being molested was our life. Maybe there were people in the country or even in the neighborhood who might have helped us if they knew what was happening, but we didn't know who they might be. As far as we knew, living like we did was "normal," how most people lived. There were plenty of other families in our barrio that fought and drank. That was how life was as far as we knew. If my mother knew what Juan was doing, she never did anything to stop him. It's hard to believe she didn't know, but I think she pretended not to know. It was easier for her and she didn't care about us.

Juan kept a supply of glue around as part of his work repairing shoes, the same kind of glue that some of the kids I knew (and I) used to inhale to get high. I was still very young then, I can't remember exactly, but maybe eight or nine. When some of my friends found out that Juan kept glue around, they talked me into taking some of Juan's glue to get high with. I didn't think anything about it at the time, other than it was something to do and when I was high I wasn't thinking about food or the rest of my awful life. From what I saw with Juan and my mother, I didn't see much difference between getting drunk and stupid and getting high and stupid from glue. One funny thing was that one of the kids I used to sniff glue with eventually ended up marrying my second daughter. But all that comes a lot later.

So my friends and I would take some of Juan's glue and go out into the "cafetales" [coffee fields] to get high away from the adults. We didn't think sniffing glue was wrong exactly, but we did know that what we were doing wasn't something we wanted adults to know about. I remember that I would take used bottles of Gerber baby food and fill them with glue from Juan's supply and sell them to the other kids. I made a little money to buy food or candy with that. So at eight or nine years old I was in business for myself! Now that I'm 47 I still sell drugs sometimes to make enough to buy food when I don't have any money. I don't buy candy any more though. I guess that's progress.

Anyway, one time I was out in the cafetal with my friends getting high on glue, and somehow my mother found us. She was really angry with me. My friends ran away but my mother dragged me home by the hair and to punish me, she gave me a "shampoo" using the glue. She poured it all over my hair and when it dried, you can imagine how it was. When she calmed down enough and the glue dried, she ended up cutting off most all of my hair. I guess I learned a lesson of some kind. That wasn't the last time I sniffed glue but it was the last time I got caught.

By the time I was maybe eleven, my mother and Juan would let me drink guaro with them. I think it was probably Juan's idea thinking that it would be easier to molest me if he got me drunk. He was always trying to touch me and Yorleny. He left Rodrigo alone. He may have been a child molester but he wasn't interested in boys. Rodrigo was lucky in that. He wasn't lucky in much, but that was one good thing.

1975 Magdalena's "School Days"

I only spent a little time in school, a few months in first grade when I was around nine years old. My mother didn't care about any of her children getting an education. School clothes and supplies aren't free *[in Costa Rica]* and the money wasn't there for school. But for some reason I did go to school a little while. Maybe a neighbor shamed my mother into it, I don't know. Anyway, I did go for a little while.

I was old enough to get myself ready, although usually there wasn't anything for breakfast and my mother and Juan were still asleep when it was time for me to go in the mornings. I usually went to school hungry. If I was lucky, we might have had some left over onions that I would fry up for myself and my brother and sister while my mother and Juan slept off their drunk from the night before. But usually I just went to school hungry.

When I went to class without eating, somehow the teacher could tell I was hungry and would share some of her lunch with me. I was very glad to have something to eat, but my classmates were jealous because they thought she was playing favorites. In my class there were three brothers, triplets actually, the only ones I have ever known in my life.

Even at that age I liked being sexy and cute. I didn't have a lot of clothes but I liked to wear my skirts short. I liked the attention, but one bad thing was that I attracted the attention of the triplets. They were always bothering me, wanting me to kiss them. It was almost like they took turns. One day it would be one of them, the next day it would be another. They wanted me to be their girlfriend, more or less... all three of them! Hah! Well I could have handled three boys but not those three. They were really fat and ugly!

Finally, one day on my way home from school they stopped me. They had their dog with them, a German shepherd. They told me they wanted a kiss, and today was the day I was going to give them a kiss. I was very small and they were big and fat, but I told them no, I didn't want to kiss any of them because they were ugly. I wasn't going to do it.

They told me that I would either kiss them, or they would sic their dog on me and have him bite me. I didn't believe they would do that. So I told them "I don't care, go ahead, your dog is better looking than you are!" I still remember the name of their dog: "Lucky." So they said "Lucky! Lucky! Bite her! Bite her!" and the dog attacked me and bit me on the leg.

I looked down at my leg and I was bleeding, so I said "Okay! Okay! I'll give you a kiss." But the school guard saw what happened and came over and took me to the school nurse, who patched me up, and the guard took the triplets to the principal's office. They were very bad kids, little monster thugs. They were still shouting at me, calling me a whore and a bitch, and saying they were going to have their dog attack me outside of the school and have him eat me!

After all that, I didn't go to school for three days. I was afraid of what they would do, the dog and the triplets. My mother and Juan didn't care one way or another. After three days my teacher sent the guard to my home to find out what was happening, why I wasn't in school. Well, my mother came out, very drunk, and told the guard that I was home because I had a fever, which was actually true because of the dog bite. She told him I didn't like school and didn't want to go. I was embarrassed because my mother was so drunk. The guard didn't know what to do so he just left.

Two days later my teacher came to the house, and my mother was drunk again, but a little less drunk than when the guard came. So my mother told my teacher that I wasn't going because I was afraid of the triplets and their dog. The teacher told my mother that I didn't have to worry because the triplets had been expelled from the school. So I put on my school uniform and left with the teacher, but she didn't take me to the school, she took me to the house where the triplets lived, to talk to their mother!

Hard to believe, but the mother was even more vulgar than her sons. She came out with a knife! The teacher told her that her sons had ordered their dog attack me. Well, instead of apologizing, she got angry! "So that's the little whore that got my sons expelled!" and she started waving the knife around and yelling "Get out of here, both of you! Get out!" So the teacher and I took off running to the school.

I went to school for maybe another month or two after that, but finally my mother told me she didn't want me to go, I think maybe it was because she didn't want to spend the money on the materials and uniforms, and because she wanted me around to help take care of my brother and sister. So that was the end of my schooling. I taught myself to read and write, but I don't do either one very well. I basically have no education. I can count but I can't really do arithmetic other than very basic adding and subtracting.

Whatever I know I learned by experience or from other people or from watching television. I love television, I watch it a lot. Newspapers and magazines are really hard for me and television is where I get my news. I have never read a book. I don't remember ever reading anything I didn't have to. It's too hard for me. Where I grew up, nobody I knew read books or even magazines and there were sure none lying around the house. Juan would sometimes bring the newspaper home to read futbol scores or look at the pictures of traffic accidents or murders. That was about it.

1979 Runaway Child Bride

My life stayed pretty much the same as it was since Mama brought Juan home until I got to be about thirteen years old. At twelve my body started to mature and by thirteen my body wasn't a little girl's body, though it wasn't quite a woman's body either. Before we reached puberty, Juan had always been trying to molest me and my sister Yorleny. Now that I was maturing, he decided that simply trying to fondle me was not enough. He told my mother that if I didn't have sex with him, he was going to leave her.

If some man I was living with had told me that, I might have tried to kill him. It didn't bother my mother, as far as I could tell. She told me that I had to let him have sex with me. I wish I could understand how she could tell me that, but I can't. The only things I can even think of are that she was afraid of losing the little money he was bringing in, or she was so in love with him she didn't want him to go, or maybe that he would get violent. But he had been violent plenty of times before so I don't think that was it.

Now, at this time I had a boyfriend named Eduardo who was eighteen. I was still a virgin and having a boyfriend was pretty innocent. When I told Eduardo what Juan and my mother had told me, what was in store for me if I kept living with them, Eduardo was shocked and very upset. He thought about it and told me we could run away to Limon together *[about 4 or 5 hours away on the Caribbean coast]*. He had friends there and they had some construction work he could do to earn some money. Although I was only twelve years old and afraid to leave home, I decided I would rather run away with Eduardo than stay and have Juan raping me night and day.

So we went to Limon together. I found out later that after I left, Juan had tried to rape my sister, Yorleny. She had gone to watch the house of a lady who lived close by. The lady had to go into town to do some errands. While Yorleny was alone in the woman's house, Juan came in and tried to rape her. The lady came back while Juan was on top of her and called the police, who came and took Juan away.

Once again, my mother chose Juan over one of her own children. She got down on her knees to Yorleny to plead with her not testify against Juan, so he wouldn't have to stay in jail. Yorleny told my mother, "Okay, I'll do that, but from now on you aren't my mother, and she left the house and never came back. She was only twelve years old at the time. She hasn't seen my mother since then.

When that happened, Eduardo and I were in Limon where he had a job and earned a little money. I was still a virgin when we left San José, although I had been masturbating for years and sexual feelings were nothing new. But the first time I had actual intercourse was with Eduardo after we got to Limon. It hurt a little the first time because I was still a virgin, physically. I had never had a penis inside me, but even though it hurt a little, I still liked it. It was maybe two weeks later that I had my first orgasm while having sex with Eduardo, my first orgasm with another person. Our sex was pretty basic, just missionary style. Not very wild, but even at twelve I liked it.

We didn't have sex all that much considering we both liked it a lot. As part of Eduardo's job on the construction crew, he was given a bunk in a barracks. There were probably about fifteen other guys in the barracks with us. So we were having sex maybe once every two or three days at the time. He was a little afraid to have sex with me because I was so young and small, and he also didn't want to get me pregnant. And sharing a little bunk bed with fifteen other men around us and a guy sleeping just above us kept us from having sex more often.

Poor Eduardo! I was still so young I was still wetting the bed. I remember wetting the bed three times when we were there sleeping together. As a child, as far back as I can remember, I was a bed wetter... from the age of six onward, from nerves I think, with all the problems at home. Eduardo was very patient and understanding with me, he knew I was still a child in most ways. I don't know if it was getting away from Juan and my mother or just growing up, but after those first three times in I wet the bed with Eduardo, I haven't wet the bed since.

We lived that way for about five months. And although we didn't know it at the time, my mother had the police looking for me and Eduardo. I don't know why she wanted me back. It's not like she cared about me. Maybe Juan told her to get me back, thinking he would get to have sex with me after all. Maybe some neighbors or family shamed her into it. It's not something I felt like asking them and they probably wouldn't have told me the truth anyway.

Eventually the police found us and brought us back to San José, me with my mother and Eduardo in the police paddy wagon. They put him in jail, and a judge gave him the choice of marrying me or staying in jail, so he married me. I'm pretty sure he would have married me anyway, since he was in love with me. So we married, even though I was still a girl in most ways. I was only thirteen then and I didn't feel I was old enough. But I only had two choices: get married to Eduardo or go back to live with my mother and be raped by Juan.

Strange as it seems, other than his sexual side, Juan is a generous and nice enough person. He's still with my mother after all these years, and has given up drinking. It may seem strange, but after Eduardo and I moved back to Desamparados [*a suburb of San José*] Juan had Eduardo help him with his shoe repairs. Maybe part of it was to free up more drinking time, but Eduardo was making at least a little money and we were able to scrape by.

1982 DIVORCED MOTHER AT 15 (1982)

Once we were back in Desamparados, Eduardo and I got a little ranchita to live in. We had water and electricity but no toilet. We lived close to my mother so when we had to we'd use her toilet. It wasn't the greatest but we were pretty accustomed to being poor. We did have a television, at least.

Although I wasn't living with my mother and Juan, I was still back around the same people as before I went away, living near most of my family and the same friends as before, the ones I used to get high with. I had a friend named Sandra who began to come over with her boyfriend Alex while Eduardo was off working with Juan. They would bring guaro, glue, paint thinner, cocaine or marijuana to get high with. There wasn't much else for me to do back then other than watch television. And getting high made watching television better, of course.

It wasn't just Sandra and Alex who came by to party and get high. And of course I didn't stay in the house all the time either, I'd go visit other people and do the same sort of things. I got plenty of attention from the guys in the barrio, including Osote, who was more or less the most respected [*feared*] guy in the barrio. I could tell he liked me, but I was faithful to Eduardo, even though I didn't really love him, not compared to what I would feel later, anyway. But I was faithful to him, so when I got pregnant, I knew who the father was. Plenty of girls I know had babies and could only guess who the father was.

After I got pregnant, I stopped doing drugs and drinking and I was pretty responsible, when you consider I was still only 13. By this time Eduardo had found out what I had been doing while he was at work, and he was upset, even though I had stopped (for the time being) because I was pregnant. And so it went until our little girl, Valeria, was born. After she was born, though, I went back to partying with my friends. Eduardo didn't like it. He came right out and asked me if I didn't love him anymore. When he put the question to me like that, I realized that I didn't love him and I told him the truth: I didn't love him and I didn't want to be married any more.

I know Eduardo loved me and that I hurt him a lot. I feel bad to think about it, but I wasn't much more than a girl. We lived together about a year after Valeria was born, but finally I moved out and we got divorced. And that's how it went. He continued to give me a little money for the baby. We didn't use disposable diapers and I breast fed Valeria, so if I kept myself fed she got fed. She didn't have a lot of clothes but there were a lot of babies around and we could usually find somebody to give her something to wear. So we scraped by.

Back in my old barrio, I didn't feel much different than before. I had a baby now, but I was still just a young teenager. Life in the barrio and with my family was still crazy. I remember one night when my sister Pati called me to tell me that my mother and Juan were drunk, as usual, and were fighting. It was so bad she was afraid they were going to kill each other. I ran over to their house and when I got there, my step father had stabbed my mother in the back, going in far enough to even reach her lung.

Pati and I took her to the hospital. Luckily the wound wasn't very serious and they released her. She could have had him sent to jail, but she said she didn't want to press charges and she just went home. But when Juan was sleeping that night, she got some rubbing alcohol and poured it over him and lit it on fire. She didn't want him to go to jail because she wanted to kill him! But rubbing alcohol isn't like gasoline and Juan wasn't badly burned... just red like a pig and with a few blisters. And before you knew it they were back drinking again and it was like nothing ever happened. Fucking drunks!

1982 A PROSTITUTE AT HOTEL EL JARDIN

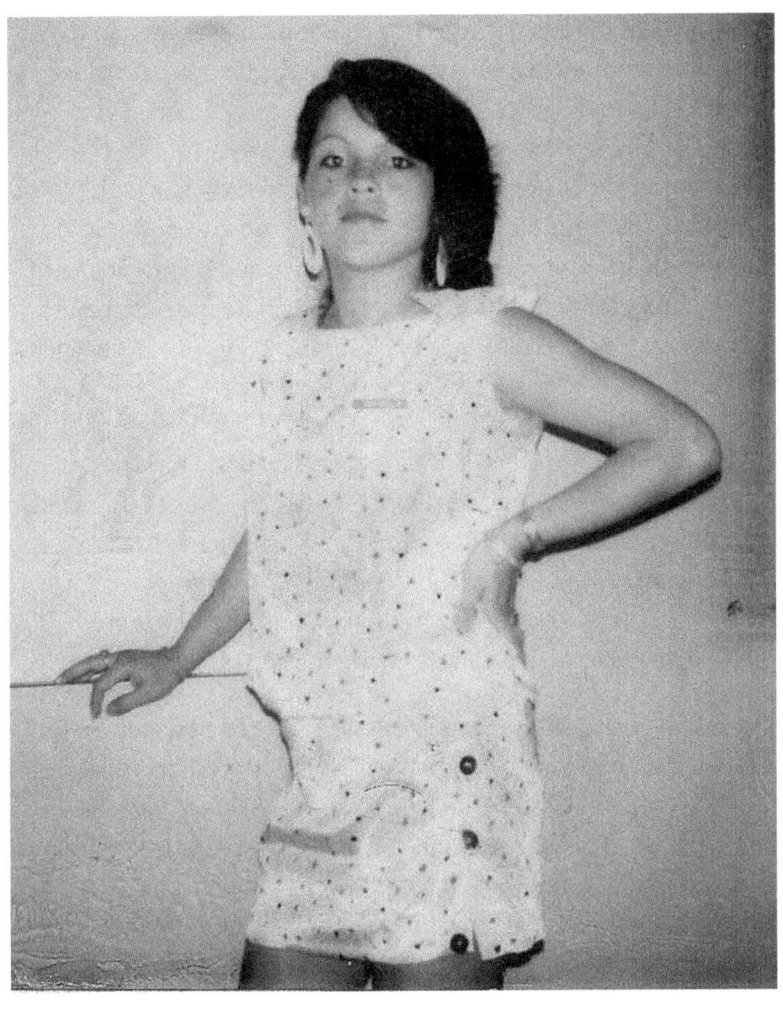

After Eduardo moved out, I was free to do whatever I wanted. I was young, cute and very popular with the guys. I liked sex and had a lot of boyfriends. They would share their mota [marijuana] with me and their beer or guaro or whatever they had and we'd have sex. I liked sex and I liked drinking and smoking mota. The sex was just part of it all.

But I was still very poor. I worked for a few weeks at an ice cream factory but I didn't like it and I hardly made any money there. One of my boyfriends, Manfred, told me about a place I could earn money just by having sex with gringos. The place was called Hotel El Jardin, and it's still pretty famous even though it's been closed for years now. Manfred said he thought I'd be better off being paid by gringos than fooling around with the local hoodlums and giving it away for next to nothing. He knew some other girls who worked there, and he knew one of the owners, not well, but a little at least. So he introduced me to Larry, who was the owner back then.

1982 LARRY

Larry was a very nice man and he treated all the girls very well. He tried to see that every girl who showed up went home with a little money. He would see sometimes one girl didn't have anybody all day and he'd talk somebody into taking her, or if there wasn't enough business some day or night he would make sure every girl left with a little money in her pocket.

Larry had very definite tastes when it came to how he wanted us to dress and make ourselves up. He insisted that we all wear really red lipstick and he insisted that we all wear low cut tops and short skirts. He liked that look and he must have thought every man liked that look. It didn't bother me because what did I know back then? The guys back in the barrio didn't need that but maybe gringos were different. I didn't know anything about gringos back then. I do now!

When Manfred introduced me to Larry, Larry told me I was very pretty, but I was very young and it was a little dangerous for me to be out where I could be seen. Because I had been married, I had applied to get my "cedula." [The Costa Rican ID card] When I had that, I could legally be in the bar, but until then, Larry said I could work there but he wanted me to stay in the kitchen, where the dishwasher and cook were. He'd bring customers back to meet me and if they wanted to be with me, we'd go upstairs to a room and have sex. I said, "Okay" and so I stayed in the kitchen until I had my cedula. I even had an apron I was supposed to put on in case the police came.

Nothing happened the first two days. I didn't get a single customer. Larry was so nice that he always gave me maybe ten dollars each those first two days. That wasn't bad at all for me. It was a lot more than I made at the ice cream factory, and that was without even doing anything!

1982 CHAPATIN

The third day he told me he had a friend who had come to town and was staying at the hotel. Larry wanted to introduce us. I said "sure, fine" and he brought the guy into the kitchen. The guy looked really strange to me. He wore a big Buck hat with a feather in it and snakeskin Buck boots. He had a big beard, was very tall and thin... I thought he looked like a Buck from the movies.

I can't remember the guy's real name but I do remember his nickname. We called him "Chapatin" because he reminded all of the girls of a character in a local soap opera, an old guy whose character was called "Chapatin." He always walked around with a cup of coffee and a cigarette. He wasn't all that old, when I think about it now, maybe fifty, but I was only fifteen so to me he seemed like such an old man, especially with that big beard and the weird way he dressed.

When we first went up to the room, I was afraid. I wasn't a virgin by any means, but it felt strange to be with a man so much older, and a gringo, too! I had never been with a gringo before. I looked at his big beard and snakeskin boots and thought to myself "Oh my God! What am I going to do? What am I going to do?" I lay down on the bed, but when he got undressed he took out a little penis and I relaxed. What did I know? I'd never been with anybody from another country. Gringos are bigger than Ticos, so I just assumed they would all have giant dicks! I was SO relieved!

So I was lying on the bed when he came to lie down next to me. He said "don't worry, don't worry, I won't do anything to hurt you." He must have sensed that I was afraid. So he lay down beside me and he just caressed me, and we didn't have sex. He gave me maybe ten dollars to spend time with him like that. We went on that way for almost a week. It was very innocent, though I wasn't innocent myself, just a little afraid of gringos. But anyway, we went on that way for about five days until one day we were drinking beer and I got pretty drunk. By that time I was also beginning to get pretty horny and Chapatin didn't scare me anymore, so we finally had sex.

After he met me, he told me I was the only girl he wanted to be with. He wanted to spend all his time with me and I think he thought of me as his girlfriend. He usually spent around three months at a time in San José then a month back in the States before he would come back again. He wasn't paying me very much for spending so much time with him, although he had lots of money. But I was new to Hotel El Jardin and I didn't know any better at first. Although he would take me shopping and buy me food, it still didn't amount to a lot when I think about all the hours I spent with him, but we went on that way for months and months.

It didn't last, of course. He wasn't always around, and when he wasn't around I got to know other men, and they paid better and they didn't expect me to spend hours and hours with them. Chapatin didn't like me seeing other men, and one day he gave me an ultimatum: if I wanted to stay with him I would have to give up all other men. If I didn't, he was going to stop seeing me. I said "Okay, bye bye," and that was that for me. But Chapatin took it pretty hard. I think he must have been in love with me. I didn't feel that way about him, though. If he thought I was in love with him, it was just his imagination or his fantasy. I never told him I was in love with him or anything like that.

Chapatin was my first customer and he was the first guy to have serious feelings for me. I didn't feel anything special for him, though. This was something that would happen quite a few times later on, guys falling in love with me that I didn't love, but Chapatin was the first. He felt a lot more for me than I felt for him. To me he was just a customer. I don't know why he thought I would want to be with him all the time.

[Q: Maybe he thought he would save you from poverty and working as a prostitute?]

I don't know what he thought. If that's what he thought, he was wrong. I didn't feel poor now that I was working. I had more money than I ever had before in my life.

[Q: What about saving you from working as a prostitute?]

I didn't ask him to save me from anything! Compared to my life before, working as a prostitute at Hotel El Jardin was the best thing that had ever happened to me. I was having fun and making money. The most boring part of my life was the time I spent with Chapatin up in his room. I liked being downstairs with the other girls and other gringos more than being with him. After I had been with some other gringos, I realized

Chapatin was cheap. He wanted a lot of my time and didn't want to pay much for it. I don't know why he thought I would give up everything to be with him.

We spent a lot of time together but he didn't really know me. He didn't know what I felt or thought. How could he? I didn't speak English and he only knew a little Spanish. He never seemed interested in my life except the time I spent with him. All he knew about me were a few basic things. He knew I was just fifteen years old with no education and that I had been very poor. He knew I liked sex and having a good time partying. That's all.

To me, gringos like Chapatin were almost from another planet. I had fun, for sure. I was making money, drinking, having lots of sex and doing some drugs. But their whole world was so different from mine. All we had in common was that we were both in Hotel El Jardin. I was barely past girlhood and I'm lying next to this big, tall, skinny, old, blond guy who wears snakeskin boots and a Buck hat with a feather in it!

Even while I was spending a lot of time with Chapatin, I never spent the night with him. I had boyfriends back in my neighborhood that were a lot sexier than Chapatin. They wouldn't have money to give me but they would have mota or something to drink and they were a lot more fun for me. Chapatin was the guy who gave me actual cash but I never felt anything special for him. Chapatin was just another strange gringo to me. My life was just happening and I was just living it.

I usually spent the evening with him from around seven until midnight. Sometimes it was in the room, sometimes in the bar downstairs. But after I left him for the night I had a life of my own. Usually I'd leave when the bar at the hotel closed. Pretty often I'd go across the street and drink some more at a bar across the street with some of the other girls. I was part of the group of girls who worked at night. The girls who worked during the day were pretty much a different group, though we knew each other, of course. But I was one of the night group.

When Hotel El Jardin's bar closed for the night we'd stay out till the sun came up sometimes. I'd go home, back to my ranchita and sleep. I had somebody to watch Valeria while I was out partying, sleeping or working. Her name was Anayetti and she was the sister in law of my sister Pati. I wasn't much of a mother to Valeria then. I was very young and my mother was no kind of example to learn from. I feel bad about it but I can't change the past.

It's been thirty years and I have met a lot of gringos since then. But when I was fifteen, it was all new to me, and the only gringos I knew were the guys who came to Hotel El Jardin. As far as I knew, they were typical of gringos everywhere. Now I realize they were a pretty strange group, not typical. But they were the only gringos I knew. There were some nice guys who seemed pretty Normal, but there were a lot of very weird guys too. I would say that probably half of them were alcoholics, or just weird in one way or another. I like to drink too and smoke mota and have a good time, but I don't start drinking the first thing every morning and drink all day and night like a lot of those guys did.

[There's a saying, popular in Costa Rica among the expatriates, that two types of gringos (single male) come here: the unwanted, and the WANTED (by the law)].

Interview with Ron – Early El Jardin Hotel

[Ron: I went there in the early days. Most of the girls were young, and they were all from Pavas or Desamparados or one of the other poor neighborhoods. There might have been twenty girls that worked there in all, and they would show up off and on... if you went there and there were ten girls working, that was a lot. It was a small, localized thing. It was set up where they would stand by the wall and if you wanted some attention you'd go over and talk to them... let's have a beer, let's go back to the room, blah blah blah. It was small... it was personalized... the girls weren't hardcore whores. They were selling their pussies to get money because they were poor. Pure and simple. All of them... it was like everybody was everybody's friend; everybody was friendly with everybody else. And they all had boyfriends. And most of the boyfriends were Eastern Airline guys, and Eastern Airlines guys knew that I'm her boyfriend this week but if Charlie gets here next week and I'm not here, Charlie is going to be her boyfriend. And there wasn't a lot of animosity in the place. It was a pretty smooth running operation.

Back then I'd say the average age of guys coming down was thirty-five to forty-five years old. There were some older and younger guys, but that was the median age. They weren't kids, rowdy and raising all kinds of shit. Back then you'd tend to see the same people. You wouldn't see the same people every trip but over the course of time you'd run into the same guys again and again.

Most of the guys back then didn't speak Spanish. Therefore, a lot of guys would come down for a month and never leave the building. They had everything they wanted there... they had a nice kitchen in the back, good meals, poker games on Saturday afternoons and all the liquor and women you'd want. And there was really nowhere else to go back then.

Where the window was on the street, there used to be a "well" there, a sunken area that would accommodate four or five guys if you squeezed them in. And it used to be great entertainment sitting down in that well, looking out at the street, looking at all the street people going by, all the ladies, all the bullshit. And then of course, on Mayday, when the communists would march with their flags and signs "Yankee Go Home" and all that, it wasn't uncommon for some of the old guys to stick their ass in the window and "moon" 'em.

There were some real characters there, Shaky Roy was one. Shaky Roy was confined to a wheel chair. He had some kind of neurological disease. I don't know what it was. But he had a pension, and Munson and Smokey would take care of all his expenses. He lived in the hotel, in his wheelchair. He had to have his eyelids taped open or he couldn't keep his eyes open. And he used to fuck with the girls. He'd just roll around in his wheelchair all day, grabbing them by the ass, grabbing their tits, spanking them... making them miserable. And there was nothing they could do about it. He was the owner's friend and he lived there. So they had to put up with him.

There was a guy we called "Puff." Puff was the only living heir of the Chriscraft fortune. And I watched him... he was an alcoholic, stone cold alcoholic... I remember he'd knock on my door at four in the morning, wake me up to take me to the Monte Carlo to get a drink. The Monte Carlo was open 24 hours, and he always had two glasses in his hands, and I thought they were water, but they were vodka. Anyway, old Puff had a gambling habit, and over the course of five or six years, I saw him gamble away his entire fortune away at the Royal Dutch hotel. So he ended up broke, and he ended up parking cars for some rental car agency in Fort Lauderdale, for a living. He got drunk and pissed off one night and shot up one of the cars and ended up in jail, and that's the last I heard of him. That had to be ten or twelve years ago. Every dime he had went to the Royal Dutch casino. It wasn't far from the El Jardin, three blocks, maybe four. He had some major problems. One, he was an alcoholic. Two, he was short. Three he was fat. Four, he was a gambler and five he didn't like to take showers. I remember him raging at Bill Munson because some girl wouldn't give him a blow job. And the girl would say "I'm not sucking that goddamn thing till he takes a shower!" He was nasty that way.

Actually, the thing about Hotel El Jardin was, if you lived there, sex was a byproduct. All the shit that went on there was about guys coming down here... from my perspective... guys who came down here to get away... to be left alone and do what they wanted to do. Now if that happened to be fucking four or five girls a day, go ahead and do it. If you want to get drunk all day, go ahead and do it. If you just wanted to be left alone, it was a place you could do it. Back when I went there, Hotel El Jardin was never a whore house. It was a bar with a hotel that allowed women to be in there, and that's basically what it was.

They had a bench in the hallway, right before the reception desk, and you'd see four or five girls sitting there. They were too young to go in the bar, but if you wanted one of them they were available. Back then it wasn't the big deal it is now, girls under eighteen. It's still no big deal except in the eyes of the law. None of these girls were virgins. Hell, most of them had babies. You ask them how old they were when they first had sex and they'll tell you thirteen, fourteen, and half the time it was their brother, step-father, whatever. It's changing a little but the farther you get out of town, the less it's changed.]

1981 EARLY YEARS IN HOTEL EL JARDIN

When I went to work at Hotel El Jardin I was only fifteen but I had been masturbating and having orgasms since I was eight, and having sex since I was 12. I didn't always like all the men who were my customers, but I was almost always able to come. If they couldn't do it for me I knew how to do it for myself.

It didn't matter how many times I went upstairs with a customer, I was almost always able to enjoy myself. But also, almost always, I would cry afterward, I was still thinking about Juan molesting me and my mother beating me if I told her not to leave me and my brother and sister alone with him. I don't know how to explain how it was that I would enjoy the sex then cry afterward. Maybe it was that I enjoyed the physical part but after it was over I had time to think, to remember, and that's when I would cry.

When I started working as a prostitute at the hotel, I was like most of the other girls there. We would drink and do drugs with the customers up in their rooms. There would be plenty to drink, lots of cocaine and marijuana and I did my share. I still like to smoke weed and do a little coke and drink, but my body can't take it now like I could when I was a teenager. I never thought I was doing anything wrong, and I wasn't much worried about the police either. They didn't bother us unless something awful happened, or somebody did something so stupid they couldn't ignore it.

Any night could be good or bad or both. Sometimes it was fun, sometimes it was sad, sometimes it was repulsive... it could be all of those in a short time, even in the same night.

There were times when I really enjoyed myself. I would drink and do cocaine and if the customer was nice looking and a nice person I liked having sex. Other times the customers were drunk, or old, or ugly or mean and it wasn't so much fun. Sometimes the men would be rough, insulting, treat me badly. They didn't hit me but sometimes the sex would be very rough, and I'm very small. When it was bad I would feel sorry for myself, and blame my mother for not taking care of me, for letting my step father abuse me, for being a drunk. I drank a lot myself, along with drugs, cocaine and marijuana. I would cry sometimes thinking of my life, and at other times I would drink and forget my problems. Sometimes I felt really bad about myself and my life, I felt like trash, garbage. And my life was full of other stresses. Sometimes it was family things, sometimes problems with friends, relationships or money. I didn't feel like I could do all that much about the problems in my life, but I could always get high and feel better about them, so I did that a lot.

My life has always been like a televovela (Latin American soap opera). I always had boyfriends and girlfriends, sometimes more than one, because I was young and pretty and almost famous, in my way. I was the star of Hotel El Jardin back then. One of my bosses used to say if he had ten like me he would have become a millionaire. I had men and women following me around and sometimes they would fall in love with me. There were places I had to avoid sometimes because I was afraid that two of my boyfriends or girlfriends would be there at the same time. I would always try to sneak a peek before I went into a bar in case there would be a problem.

There were times when I would have a couple of men or women in love with me at the same time. I never wanted that and I never led them on, but I DID like sex and the men would pay me and I needed the money so I didn't tell them to go away. I never lied to them, I always tried to tell them I didn't want a relationship, that I wanted to be free, but they didn't listen. I didn't want to hurt anybody but I couldn't stop them from being foolish.

The truth is that my nature is like a butterfly, I don't like to be tied down. I would tell my customers and lovers this, and if they didn't mind sharing me then we could get along, but if they wanted me to be their own, they should forget me.

But I also drank because I liked to party and have fun. It wasn't all just because my life was bad sometimes. I would drink every night, only guaro, always guaro. I was young and I recovered quickly from drinking so much. I would drink for the fun of it and I would drink to help me forget the bad parts of my life. But either way, I drank a lot of guaro and did a lot of cocaine and smoked a lot of weed. I still do, but not like before. I'm a grandmother now, forty seven years old and with nine grandchildren! My body can't take that pace any more. I have to go a little easier.

1983 NEW OWNER - NEW LOVER

About the same time that I stopped with Chapatin, I started going with Bill Munson, who was the new owner after Larry. Bill was about fifty he was married to a Tica who was maybe ten or fifteen years younger than he was. *[A "Tica" is a Costa*

Rican woman. Men are called "Ticos."] She was nice looking and classy, but I was a lot younger and I could tell as soon as I met Bill that he was attracted to me.

Bill and his wife lived together in Escazú *[a rich suburb of San José]* most of the time, but she liked to travel a lot, especially to the United States. Bill was rich and had a house in the United States too. She went there pretty often. She liked it there and everybody in the bar was sure she had a lover up there and that's why she went to the States so often. Nobody knew for sure, of course, but we loved to gossip.

After I was done with Chapatin, and Bill's wife went on one of her visits to the United States, I started seeing Bill. It was obvious to me and all the girls that Bill liked me. He was very nice to everybody but a little nicer to me than the other girls. When his wife left, one thing led to another and after a week or so we went up to one of the rooms and had sex. We both enjoyed it, and we did the same thing every night for maybe two weeks. After that, he had me come to stay with him in his house in Escazu. This was while his wife was still in the States, of course. Eventually, whenever his wife was on one of her trips, I would go stay with him instead of in the hotel or back in Desamparados. We carried on like that a long time. Whenever his wife would be about to come back I'd take my things out and go back to the hotel, while he cleaned up and made sure there was no evidence for her to find.

While this was going on, my daughter stayed with my sister Pati sometimes and sometimes with a neighbor I trusted, and sometimes with me. All of us lived close together so maybe she'd spend the morning at a neighbor's and the afternoon and night with Pati or spend the afternoon with me and the night with the neighbor.

I saw Valeria pretty often, three or four days a week would be the average even when I was staying at Bill's. I didn't think a lot about whether I was being a good mother or not back then. I was a lot better to her than my mother was to me! Nobody ever touched my children and they never went hungry or without clothes. They all went to school. That's more than my mother can say. But now that my children are grown I wish I had paid them more attention, especially Valeria and Gloriana. I was more mature with my son and I paid him more attention. Valeria and I aren't even speaking now. I wish we were closer but I am afraid it's too late.

I got along very well with Bill. He was a very generous and kind man. At Christmas he would hold a big party for all the children of all the girls that worked there, and buy them all presents and have cake and ice cream and all kinds of things. He would have somebody dress up like Santa Claus and hand out presents. The bar was open to all the girls and their kids. Everybody had a great time. He was very good to us all. He even hired a private tutor to try to teach all the girls English. Most everybody who worked there at the time could speak basic English after a while.

While I was staying with Bill off and on, I was also working at the hotel when his wife was in town and still fooling around with the guys in the barrio where I was living. One of them was a guy called "Osote," (big bear) and he was basically the more respected [feared] guy in the barrio. He was in his twenties and I suppose I was proud that the "boss" of the barrio liked me. I knew him pretty much all my life but we only began fooling around after I divorced Eduardo. Back then, around the time I started working at Hotel El Jardin, he was just one of the guys I was having sex with and I was just one of his girlfriends. We weren't serious to begin with. That came a little later.

Hotel El Jardin was a very wild place. One of the things I remember was the blow job contests Bill used to have. He would offer a prize to the girl who was voted best at giving head by the gringos who volunteered to be the "judges." Every girl got paid something for joining in the contest, but the winner would get enough to take the night off and go home with as much as she might earn on a good night.

Bill liked that kind of thing, and the customers liked it too. That's no surprise. And none of us girls had to do it if we didn't want to, but it was money and there was a certain rivalry between us too. As far as I can remember, I used to win more often than anybody else, which didn't help me being popular with some of the other girls, but I didn't care. To me it was something I was proud of. It was my job and I was good at it! Each of us girls would give head to each of the customers who volunteered and they would judge who was the best. Whoever got the most votes won the big prize, but all the girls got something. It was a good time to work there.

But it wasn't always perfect. Since I was the boss' favorite, there was a lot of jealousy and there were always girls who didn't like me too much. It was my own fault sometimes. In Costa Rica, and in San José especially, there are two football [soccer] teams that are the most popular. Almost everybody prefers either Saprissa or Liga de Alajuela. My favorite team is Liga. I am a "Ligista." So one night it was the big game between Saprissa and Liga. Usually Bill didn't like to have football on because the gringos didn't like it and they were our customers. But that night we all begged him to let us watch the match, and he gave in. So the game was played and Saprissa won. Like I say, I am a "Ligista," and as usual there was a lot of rivalry between the Saprissa girls and the Liga girls. After Liga lost, a couple of the Saprissa girls were giving me a hard time about it, teasing me. I feel stupid now, but I got so mad I attacked one of the Saprissa girls and began to punch her in the face. Well, I guess I got what I deserved when she picked up a beer bottle and hit me in the face with it, right near my left eye. It hurt like a sonofabitch and I ran off, crying. My eye healed up pretty well in about a week, but I had trouble with that eye for years afterward. My eye would water and I'd have to carry around a napkin to wipe it.

Bill's wife was very bossy. She was a very elegant looking lady, but bossy. It was weird enough living in their house when she was away in the United States, but probably the weirdest thing that happened during that time was when his wife told Bill she wanted to do a threesome with him and me! She had no idea that I had been living with him while she was gone, and it felt really weird to me, but I didn't feel like saying "no." I was AFRAID to say "no." So I said "yes" and all three of us had sex together. She was very much the boss. She had me go down on her and she liked it. She was very clean, though, and it never bothers me to do that if the other girl is clean. Of course, I like it better to GET than GIVE, but I didn't mind licking her, other than how weird it was with her not knowing about Bill and me.

I was still spending time in Desamparados during the time I was with Bill. Bill was very good to me, but when his wife was in town I spent most of my time in Desamparados, partying with people about my own age in what we called a "bunker," which was a little shack that belonged to Manuel, one of the small-time drug dealers in the neighborhood. The "bunker" was a place where we could do drugs and drink in private.

I didn't really have much in common with Manuel except I thought he was sexy and we did drugs and drank together in the bunker. But me being horny and a little slip led to me getting pregnant with my second daughter, Gloriana. I was a little worried about how Bill would react, but he didn't mind at all. I kept on staying with him when his wife was away and when I got too pregnant for sex with him, he still took care of me. I had the baby and I was able to go back to work almost right away because all of my babies were Caesarean. I'm very tiny and the doctors thought it was best. Valeria was five or six by then and I was nineteen.

I was still with Bill after Gloriana was born, but the other girls had always been jealous of me being his favorite, and there was a lot of gossip going around that said Gloriana was Bill's baby. It wasn't true, but gossip is gossip. Bill was still very good to me. He had somebody take a picture of us together while he was holding Gloriana. And he put it up on the wall over the bar. This turned out to be a big mistake.

His wife used to come to the hotel and hang around whenever she was in town. Nobody liked it because it wasn't the same when she was around. Bill wasn't any fun and we all felt inhibited around her. So one day when she was there, she noticed the picture of the three of us. One of the girls, I don't know who, but one of them told her that Gloriana was Bill's baby. She wasn't, but it didn't matter whether or not she was Bill's. When somebody told his wife that we had been fooling around, that was enough to put an end to our affair. The wife told him he could either sell the bar or they would get a divorce. He decided to sell the bar, and that was the end of my time with Bill.

Another New Owner and Lover

Because I am so small, I had all my babies by Caesarean. So it wasn't long after Gloriana was born that I went back to work at Hotel El Jardin. When his wife made him sell the bar, Bill sold it to a man named Dave. Dave had been around the hotel for quite a while, and when he took over the bar it's almost like I was part of the deal. I'm sure there wasn't any agreement between Bill and Dave, but it did just turn out that as soon as Bill was gone, I started seeing Dave. Dave was even older than Bill, maybe 60, but still handsome. He fell in love with me really fast, too fast. He didn't want me to work at the hotel any more so he rented us a really nice house in Rohrmoser, a really nice part of town. He wanted me to just stay home and take care of my girls. And I did, more or less. I didn't work at the hotel any more, but I was still young and wild and loved to party.

He was in love with me, and I liked him very much, though I wasn't in love. But we fought a lot. It was because both of us were jealous, and because of my drinking and liking to party. Dave didn't drink, and he didn't like me drinking. I didn't like him telling me what to do. He was jealous of other guys and I was jealous of all the girls in Hotel El Jardin. He would be down at the hotel and I would be in the house and he would always be calling to check up on me, asking me what I was doing, as if I was having sex with some guy and as if I would tell him if I was! He was just too obsessed with me. When he wasn't at the hotel, he wanted to spend all day in bed. I like sex a lot, but not twenty four hours a day!

I felt like a prisoner or a hostage... I wasn't free. I was young and pretty and loved life and people. I loved to flirt and I loved being the star of Hotel El Jardin. And he knew this and it made him even more jealous. We'd argue and sometimes it would get physical. I remember one time he wanted to hit me but I got him first and gave him a black eye!

He finally had enough of the fighting and arguing, and me drinking and going wild, and he broke up with me. He was still friendly, but he found somebody else to be his girlfriend. It was okay with me because I was ready to be free again, to do what I wanted without anybody to tell me what to do.

LIFE WITH OSOTE

Right after I got divorced, and even before I started working at Hotel El Jardin, I was seeing a lot of different guys in the neighborhood and having sex with them. Like I said before, I like sex and never seem to get enough. Or I can get enough for a while but it's not long till I want to do it again. Osote was one of the guys I was having sex with.

Osote was the most respected man in our neighborhood. When I say he was respected, I don't mean like I would respect a saint or the president, but he was feared and nobody messed with him. I was proud that he liked me and wanted me to be his girlfriend. It didn't happen all at once, but I ended up living with him, at least when he wasn't in jail and we weren't fighting. But I still spent a fair amount of time in Hotel El Jardin, since he kept going to jail or we'd fight and I'd go party with my friends there and maybe work to make some money.

He wasn't the only feared member of his family. His mother was very well known for being violent and dangerous. She would get into fights all the time with the neighbor women. And they weren't just arguments, they were physical fights and

Osote's mother would beat them up. She was a big woman and looked like a dyke, though she wasn't a lesbian as far as I know. The neighbor women had husbands and boyfriends but even they were afraid of Osote's mother. Maybe they could have won a fight with her, but they knew she had a gun and a machete and she was crazy enough to use them. And later on, of course, there was Osote to deal with. Anybody who touched his mother had to answer to him, and nobody wanted to do THAT.

When I first started seeing him, I was around sixteen and Osote was quite a bit older, twenty eight maybe. He made his money from selling marijuana and robbing houses. Back then he sold the strongest marijuana you could get anywhere. He would sell other things too. He sold glue that he got at the hardware store and whatever he could get his hands on. He also robbed people's houses, along with my brother Rodrigo and a lesbian named Doris.

Osote liked to take pills, different kinds, whatever he could get, it seemed to me back then. One of his favorites was Akineton [generic name Biperedin, used to treat Parkinson's disease as well as depression and other conditions. When taken in large enough quantities it can produce euphoria and hallucinations along with many other potentially dangerous side-effects]. Of course there was lots of "mota" [marijuana] and he drank a lot of Abuelo rum [an expensive local brand]. He used to insist that I drink and take pills with him. He loved it all but I didn't. I liked getting high, but not with all the different drugs he wanted me to do with him. I felt like I was living in slow motion. I felt like a slug. But even though I didn't like doing all those drugs, I did them anyway because it was part of living with Osote. I was maybe 85 lbs, soaking wet. Telling Osote "no" wasn't something I did very often. It wasn't something ANYBODY did very often.

It's no surprise that Osote and I had a very unstable relationship. It would have been a miracle if we didn't. There were a lot of things I didn't like about things he did. I didn't mind the "mota" and a little cocaine, and I didn't mind a little rum or beer, but he did too many different things and too much of everything. I liked to get high to the point I was just having fun, but he kept going and going until he was out of his mind. He took everything to the limit. Even with sex, he liked to do things I just didn't like, like spit in my mouth. He liked it, I hated it. The first time I put a penis in my mouth it was Osote's. He was older and much more experienced than Eduardo. He taught me a lot about sex, including the whole oral thing. It wasn't my idea, but he wanted it so I did what he wanted even though it seemed unsanitary to me at first. But after about a month I was enjoying it. And he was the first man to go down on me, lick my pussy, and I loved it right away. So it was only natural I would do the same for him and it wasn't long before I got to like giving head. I still like giving head, but I like getting head more!

A STRANGE LOVE NEST

Back before I moved in with Osote, I noticed that his brother Pedro, was interested in me. The attraction was mutual. I was crazy, young and crazy. He wanted me and I wanted him, but the last thing we wanted was for Osote to find out. We weren't living together yet, but we both knew Osote wouldn't like it. So Pedro said that he would find a place we could do it and nobody would know. That sounded good to me.

One day he came over to where I was staying and said he had found a place. I asked him where but he wouldn't tell me, he just said it would be a surprise. He wasn't joking! So anyway, it was just a little past dark and off we went. I thought we were going to a hotel or something like that.

So we started walking, and I thought it was a little strange that we were walking through coffee fields. After a little while we were standing in a little spot behind a church in Desamparados. It's all been built up now, but there were open space back then. Anyway, it was dark and there was nobody around. I asked him how much farther and he said "right here!"

I have to say I was a little shocked, or at least surprised. Obviously there wasn't a bed there. There wasn't even a bench or a seat. But I was horny, like always, so when Pedro spread his jacket on the ground, I took my clothes off and we began to go at it. I remember thinking how good it was, and I was almost ready to come when I felt something strange, like something crawling on my skin. I looked down and saw I was being attacked by these black ants, the kind that bite. I started shouting "Pedro! Pedro! I'm being eaten alive by ants!" So I jumped up in a rush, furiously trying to brush off the ants. I saw this as a sign from God that we shouldn't be fucking behind the church and that's what I told Pedro. I told him we should stop. God must be angry! Pedro thought otherwise. He told me he was going to finish what he started and pushed me back against the wall of the church and after a few more minutes of energetic fucking, we both came.

Once it was over I started to feel afraid. I felt sure that God would punish me for having sex behind one of his churches, and on top of that I knew Osote would have been furious if he knew what I did, with his OWN BROTHER even! Luckily it was two years before he found out and I wasn't with Osote any more.

While we were together, it seemed like there was always some kind of trouble. I remember one day when it was my birthday, maybe my sixteenth, I'm not sure. But I was fighting with Osote, and Doris said we should go into San José and celebrate. I said sure. So I went with her to a bar near the big black bank on Second Avenue [Bank of Costa Rica]. This was a long time ago and there was a little bar near there. I had put on this white dress with a ruffled skirt that spread out like a sunflower. The bar was called the Soda del Banco and it was considered very dangerous. But danger and violence were nothing new to me, so I went with Doris and a couple of local hoodlum types to celebrate my birthday.

Even before we left Desamparados, we were pretty high. We had all been taking a lot of different pills. I don't remember what they were and I'm not sure we knew what they all were when we took them. When we got to the bar, Doris found us a table. But when I went to sit down at the table, some drunk pulled the chair out from under me and I fell on the ground. When Doris saw this she pushed the guy to the ground and began kicking him in the head. I grabbed a bottle and broke it across the table and started stabbing him with the broken bottle.

If we weren't all messed up, we probably wouldn't have gone that crazy. I don't think I would have, but we were and before I knew it my pretty, new, white dress was smeared all over with blood. Although we were fucked up, we still realized that police would be coming pretty soon so we took off out of there, running down the street as fast as we could. As I ran, people we passed stared at me and my new white dress all covered with blood and I overheard them saying "that poor little girl is hurt!" They had no idea it wasn't my blood, but the blood of the guy I stabbed with a broken beer bottle. I feel bad about it when I think about it. I think I cut him pretty bad. I was lucky not to have killed him, as high and crazy as I was. He was pretty lucky too, since he could have died for the sake of a stupid joke. They say a cat has nine lives. I think I must have more than that, considering all the violence I've seen and been a part of. I have knife scars and even bullet wounds to prove it.

A SHOOTOUT

One night Osote and I were in our "ranchito" when his burglary partner Pablito came over to get Osote to go do a burglary. I wasn't keeping track, but I'd say they would do this two or three times a week. They would take a crowbar to pry open the doors or the bars on the windows. They left just a little after dark, a little after six pm I would guess. They came back at around ten or eleven with a television, a music system, a microwave oven, some jewelry and assorted other things. So as they were dividing up the "loot," we did what we usually did: we drank rum, smoked some mota, and snorted some cocaine. It wasn't too long before we were all pretty messed up. At some point Pablito went to the bathroom and left his jacket in the room. Osote didn't totally trust Pablito, so he went over to check the pockets of Pablito's jacket, and he found a bunch of jewelry there... rings, earrings, necklaces, that sort of thing. Their agreement was that they would all share equally in whatever they got, but it looked like Pablito was holding out on Osote.

When Pablito came out of the bathroom, Osote confronted him: "Why do you have all this jewelry in your jacket?!? We're supposed to split everything! You're ripping me off!"

Pablito answered "No man! That jewelry belongs to my mother!" Yeah, right.

"Your mother? How the hell can this be your mother's, she lives 150 miles away in Guanacaste! Do you think I'm an idiot?"

"No man, I swear these are my mother's!"

Well, Osote didn't believe a word of this, and he took off to get his revolver, which he kept next door where his mother lived. Pablito took off to his own house as soon as Osote was gone to get HIS gun. These guys weren't fooling around. I knew something really bad was going to happen.

Pablito was gone when Osote came back with his pistol. He was drunk and drugged and looked like a zombie. He went out into the street and started shouting at Pablito: "You motherfucking bastard, you aren't going to rip me off like that. Give me that jewelry right now or I'll blow you away!"

"You'll have to kill me first, unless I kill YOU!" Pablito answered.

I'm hearing all this from inside the "ranchito." All of a sudden I hear "boom boom!" And like an idiot, I go outside to look and there was Osote around the corner of one ranchito and Pablito around the corner of another, maybe 20 meters apart, shooting at each other. I stayed in the doorway, out of the way, tried to talk to Osote.

"Osote, this is crazy, you're going to kill your friend!"

"He's no friend of mine, that dick-face bastard! We're supposed to share and that fucker ripped me off! I'm not going to let him get away with that!"

So there I was, trying to stay out of the way while Osote and Pablito were shooting at each other. I don't know how many shots were fired, but quite a few. I guess they were lucky they were both so fucked up they didn't hit each other. But there was a bum out in the streets at the time and one of the bullets hit him in the leg.

"Oh fuck, fuck! My leg, my leg!" he shouted. Well, who knows how it would have ended if the bum hadn't gotten shot, but somebody must have called the police when the shooting started, because we could hear the sirens coming. So Osote did what he always did when he was running away from the police, he climbed up on the roof and ran across the roofs to escape.

[Note: in Costa Rica most houses, especially in poor neighborhoods, are built side by side, no space between them, and most are one story]

So Osote took off one way and Pablito took off in another direction. When the police came, both the shooters were gone and nobody around seemed to know who was doing shooting. There wasn't much the police could do but call for an ambulance to take the bum to the hospital.

I didn't see Osote until the next day, when he came back covered in mud. Pablito never came back to the barrio at all. He just disappeared. We figured he probably went back to Guanacaste where his mother lived. A few years later we heard that Pablito was in jail, and while he was in there somebody killed him. I don't know why or how it happened. I just heard that somebody killed him.

MORE VIOLENCE

Osote's best friend, Diego, had a girlfriend who was the daughter of an older man who was also well respected *[feared]* in the barrio. The father didn't like the fact that his daughter was going with Diego because they were "bad" people... criminals, drug users, all that. Of course the father was anything but a saint himself, but that didn't matter. He was very angry with Diego and determined that his daughter not be involved with him. He wasn't looking for trouble but he didn't want his daughter to have anything to do with Osote and his friend.

That was the situation one day when Osote and I were in the ranchito having sex. We heard men shouting outside and heard one say to the other: "Listen, you motherfucker, stay away from my daughter!" We recognized the voice of the father.

"Your daughter loves me, she's going to be with me whether you like it or not!" Diego shouted back.

When people back then didn't use guns they fought with machetes, and they would bang their machetes against the pavement before they fought. Sometimes they wouldn't fight but they would always hit the pavement with the machetes to start with. When Osote and I heard the sound of machetes hitting the pavement we stopped what we were doing, put on some clothes and hurried outside.

What we saw was terrible. Diego was standing with one hand almost completely cut off, just dangling by some skin or tendons or something. And the father's arm was cut badly too, half cut off at least.

I told Osote, "Please don't get in the middle of this, it isn't your problem!"

He said, "But they are both my friends, I can't let them kill each other! They are almost dead. One lost his hand and the other lost his arm!"

Diego's mother came running and began shouting at her son, "Diego! Diego! Come with me! We need to get to the hospital! Come on!"

Diego pushed his mother away,

"That fucker cut my hand off, I'm going to kill him!" and when he pushed his mother, she fell to the ground because she was very old and weak. When Osote saw this, he got very angry and took out his pistol and fired it in the air: Pow! Pow!

"Listen to me, you dick heads! You almost killed each other and I won't let you hurt the old woman. Stop it right now or I'll shoot you both!"

And like before, the police came and called an ambulance, this time to take Diego and the father to the hospital. And also like before, Osote took off across the rooftops and escaped.

Breaking Up With Osote

Things went on with Osote and me for a year or so. We would break up and get back together. When we weren't together I'd go back to the El Jardin to make money. We had a rocky relationship, to say the least. I really didn't like Osote's lifestyle. I was no saint, but living with Osote was much too crazy for me. One time when we broke up he was so shook up he actually tried to kill himself by stepping in front of an ice cream truck. What a way to go, eh? He was very fucked up on some mixture of drugs, I'm sure. He was lucky though. The truck wasn't going that fast and it didn't kill him. It didn't even do him all that much harm, just a lot of bruises and a cracked rib.

We finally split up for good because I just couldn't take living like that anymore, so I found a place where my two girls and could live. It was just a ranchita but I got away from the worst of Osote's craziness.

JAILBIRD

One thing I got from my time with Osote was a group of contacts in the drug world, people who dealt in drugs. I began to sell cocaine and I didn't work all that much at the El Jardin because I preferred selling drugs. It's not that I didn't like sex anymore; it was just that I had more freedom to do what I wanted when I wanted.

One evening I went with a few friends to this bar to party, dance and sell some cocaine. We were sitting and talking and drinking and this man came over and asked me to dance. Well, I loved to dance, but I told him no. I told him I didn't know how. Of course I knew how, I just didn't feel like dancing right then, and not with HIM even if I did. But he wouldn't take no for an answer. He kept insisting, and I kept repeating that I didn't know how. Finally after the fourth or fifth time, he got really angry with me and punched me right in the face. I guess some girls would have run away, but whenever I'm attacked or threatened, I get really angry. I got so mad that I broke a beer bottle on the table and slashed his face, cut him pretty good with the broken bottle. When I saw all the blood, though, I got really frightened and fainted to the ground. When I awoke I was in a holding cell at the police station. I spent the night there and the net morning they took me to "Buen Pastor." *[The "good shepherd," the prison for women]* You can imagine how afraid I was, still just a teenager getting put into that filthy prison with all the older woman criminals. It was awful.

Being so young and small, I was pretty helpless against almost any of the women in there who wanted to hurt me. One of the inmates, an ugly dyke named "Maria Felix" was attracted to me. Her way of showing it was to say disgusting things to me such as "Baby, I'm going rape you" or "I'm going to lick you." When she said "rape" she meant with a broomstick.

[Apparently this is not uncommon in Costa Rican prisons and jails, for both males and females. It may be common elsewhere but I haven't heard of it except from Magdalena.]

Finally, one day, she did try to rape me, with the broom. I would have been no match for her, but there was another woman there who stepped in to protect me. Her name was "Fabi" *[short for Fabiola]* and I considered her my best friend in the jail. Eventually she seduced me, so I guess maybe her reasons for protecting me weren't totally unselfish. But she did save me, and treated me kindly. And as far as the seduction went, I was so horny that day I just let her go ahead. Ever since then I have had sex with women more times than I can remember. I call myself a lesbian and prefer to have a girlfriend than a boyfriend, but I still like sex with men too.

But my first time with a woman was with Fabi. After she saved me from Maria Felix, we went to my cell and Fabi asked me if I was okay, and I said yes, and thanked her. She said she did it because she was older and bigger and wasn't going to let anybody hurt me. I was young and pretty and she wasn't going to let anybody harm me. I thanked her again and she asked me if I was married, or had a boyfriend. I knew what she was getting at. I told her no, I didn't have a husband or boyfriend, but I wasn't interested in women. She asked me how I knew since I had never tried? I told her I didn't want to. I was afraid.

The way it was in Buen Pastor is that you could pay other women to guard the door if you wanted to be alone with somebody. The guards were actually nuns, and they were usually horrible to us, treated us like shit. Most of the nuns were very strict and mean but there were others you could bribe. So one afternoon Fabi arranged for us to have some privacy in my cell. I remember she brought me a really nice wristwatch as a present, in a really pretty case. I was only sixteen at the time and there weren't many times in my entire life anybody had got me a present, especially something really nice like this.

So there we were, and I felt really emotional about her giving me this present. Even though I had never tried anything with a woman before and I was afraid, at the same time I was curious and horny. After all, it wasn't going to kill me and she had been so nice to me, I didn't really mind. She started very slowly, just massaging my neck, holding my hand, stroking my arm. Then she began to kiss my neck, little kisses. She started nice and slowly, but in a little while she was taking off my uniform, what we all wore in jail, and when she went down on me with her tongue, I liked it a lot. And after that we were girlfriends.

Having sex in the jail wasn't easy to do, but Fabi was able to arrange it because some of the nuns could be bribed and she had help from her friends, too. She had been in jail for quite a while and had a lot of influence. I guess you could call her one of the leaders, kind of like Osote was back in the barrio. So we were able to be together pretty often.

I ended up spending three months in prison before my mother was able to get some money together to get me out, post bail for me. I was happy she did that, but it's not like she changed all of a sudden. She never did anything for me when I was a little girl. The fact is that I was doing pretty well between working at Hotel El Jardin and selling drugs. Before I went to jail I was giving her some money, and I'm pretty sure that's why she bothered getting me out: to get the money rolling her way again.

FREE AGAIN

Even though she never seemed to care about me, I can't help caring about her. She's my mother. Sometimes I just wish I could get a hug from her, when I feel down. I cry sometimes when I think how much I need her and how she doesn't care about me. I know there's nothing I can do but that's just how I feel.

Anyway, I was only doing three months, and Fabi was doing three years. When I got out she still had seven months left to serve. We were girlfriends in jail but when I got out I was back on my own. I had a girl from Guanacaste who had been taking care of Valeria and Gloriana for me while I was in jail, and I moved in with them and went back to working at Hotel El Jardin again, along with a little drug dealing on the side. I might even have gone back with Osote, but while I was in jail the police got him again for a robbery, and he was in jail when I got out, so I was on my own.

Osote had been in and out of jail quite a few times, but during that last stretch he ended up killing a transvestite for some reason or other and got fourteen years for it. He finally got out years later, but by that time we didn't really have anything in common. My life was very different. And after he got out of jail, he only spent a year and a half outside before somebody murdered him. I don't know who it was, but he definitely had plenty of enemies. I was sad to hear it, but I wasn't surprised. He lived a violent life, and that's how he died.

BACK TO HOTEL EL JARDIN

All the time I was with Osote, I would still go to Hotel El Jardin. Sometimes I would just go to party with my friends and sometimes, when we were fighting or separated for a while, I'd go there to work too. It was only natural that when I got out of jail I went back there to work.

Plenty of strange things happened in Hotel El Jardin. One thing I can't forget is when a group of us girls were sitting around downstairs waiting for customers and one of the guys who was staying at the hotel came down from upstairs with this giant snake in his hands! I have no idea what kind it was, but it was REALLY big, like a boa constrictor, or that's how it looked to us, anyway. We were all terrified but the guy wasn't afraid. He had found it when he was looking for something in his closet. Who knows how long that snake had been up there, but it was BIG, so I think it must have been hiding upstairs there for a long time. It was funny when it was all over. The guy paid a taxi driver to drive it out to the country and set it loose. But you should have heard us all screaming when we saw him come down the stairs with that snake!

A lot of the gringos who came to Hotel El Jardin were drug users. There was a lot of cocaine, marijuana, and all kinds of pills. Most of the time I didn't know what they were taking, but I don't think it was vitamins . One day a gringo came in and he spoke some Spanish, and he wanted me to go back with him to his apartment. I told him I never left the hotel with anybody because I was young, underage, and I was afraid. He said not to worry, that he was a friend of the owner and I could trust him, nothing bad would happen. But I looked at his arms, and they were covered with marks, and I thought how strange it was. But he told me not to worry; he wasn't going to do anything to hurt me. So I told him I'd go but he had to leave his name, address, passport number and so on with the bar, so they would know who I left with. I thought if everybody knew we left together he would be afraid to do anything because they would know who he was. He said sure, no problem, and gave the bartender all his information. He told me he was going to give me $30, which was quite a bit back then for me. So we left for his apartment.

When we got to his apartment, there was a little table and on top of it were a bunch of needles and syringes. This scared me a little and he said not to be afraid, they were for him, not for me. I asked him if he was sick and he said no, that he used heroin. And I said "But isn't that a drug?" and he said "of course," So I asked him if he could have sex with that drug and he told me he didn't want to have sex with me, he just wanted me to hang out with him. He just wanted me to get naked, and him get naked, and we'd lie down together and I'd suck him. Well, I was still afraid, but he gave me another $20 to make me feel better and I said to myself okay, I might as well give it a try, see how it went.

Time went on and he was giving me $10 more, then $10 more. And when he gave himself an injection, for five minutes his dick would get hard, then after the five minutes it would get limp again. He kept doing this, but he was sweating like a pig and pale as a ghost, and it really scared me. My God! What if this guy dies on me right here? That's how bad he looked. He noticed that I looked scared and he asked me if he was sweating and looked pale, and I said yes, he looked like he was going to die. Again he told me not to worry, he was used to this, it was normal for him. I told him maybe so but I wasn't used to it.

"Don't worry, don't worry," he told me, "I've been doing this for ten years."

"But you're spending a ton of money," I told him.

"It doesn't matter," he answered, "The Devil has been very good to me. He gave me a lot of money." So I was with him something like five hours, and in that time he gave me around $200 dollars, which was a fortune for me. And for the next three days he came looking for me because he liked me, so I could have made a lot of money, but I had another gringo who showed up and he was somebody that I thought I might get serious about, so I told him I couldn't be with him. He was disappointed but asked me if I had another girl that was fun and would like to spend time with him, somebody like me. I told him there was nobody like me and he laughed and said yes, he understood, but could I introduce him to somebody nice? I had a friend Vicki and so I introduced them and they spent time together. I didn't stay close to Vicki, but I heard years later that she died of AIDS. I don't know that it had anything to do with the drug addict but she died before she was forty. Anyway, I never saw the gringo again. I went to the beach with the other gringo for a few days and when we came back he was gone and never came back. Who knows what happened?

KLAUS, THE CAT KILLER

There were a lot of strange gringos who came through Hotel El Jardin back then. I remember there was this one gringo, a German named John, who lived in a nice apartment down near Hospital Mexico. He was pretty strange; he was always taking pills of one kind or another. I don't know what he was taking but he was very thin. Whenever he would show up at the El Jardin, all the girls would flock around him because he would pay each of us $100! That's good money now but back then it was a MOUNTAIN. He always wanted three or four women and he always carried a pistol. He was always afraid, he thought people were following him, what they call paranoid.

One time I was up in the room with him and another girl and while I was in the shower, I heard the gun go off. I ran out of the shower, dripping wet, and saw that the other girl was shaking. Apparently there had been a cat outside the window that was making noise and bothering him, and he got so upset he shot it! We told him that he needed to leave right away because you just don't do that in Costa Rica. The police would come and you never know what they will do; maybe take him to jail, maybe try to get a bribe. He left and the police did come around but since there was nobody there to get a bribe from, they left.

He just stopped coming to Hotel El Jardin and I didn't see him for a really long time. Then one day I saw him one last time just a few years ago in the New York Bar. He told me he had paid some Ticos [*Costa Ricans*] to get him residency but they just took the money and disappeared. He told me he was leaving Costa Rica for good and nobody I know has seen him since.

THE MAN ON CRUTCHES

Another time, I was sitting at a table Hotel El Jardin with some of the other girls when this gringo came in. We all paid attention whenever a gringo came in. We would check him out, see what he looked like, see who he might be interested in. I noticed that he was walking with crutches but I thought maybe he had an accident or something. I didn't think all that much about it.

This happened not long after I started at the El Jardin. I was very young and flirtatious. I had become quite popular, so I wasn't surprised when he noticed me and called me over to sit with him at the bar. He offered me a drink and asked me my name and asked how much I charged. I told him and he said, okay, and that he would give me a tip because he said there was something strange about him but that it was nothing I should be afraid of, nothing that would harm me. I told him not to worry, that I was used to strange things, that I had been with drunks and crazy men before and I wasn't worried. He asked me "Are you sure?" and I told him yes, let's go to the room.

When we got to the room, I went into the bathroom to shower, like I always do. And also like I did back then, I did a little coke and smoked a little bit of weed to get me "in the mood." When I came out I was naked with just a towel around me, but he was sitting on the bed with his clothes on, and he seemed uncomfortable. He said he was going to take off his clothes, and I joked that it was a good idea since we couldn't have sex if he had his clothes on.

He smiled but at the same time he seemed very uneasy. So he took off his shirt and took off his pants. And I noticed his legs were a different color than the rest of him. They were plastic... artificial. I guess my face must have shown my shock, because he told me please not to leave him because he really wanted to be with me. I told him I was just a little afraid because I was surprised. So he took off one of his legs, and then the other leg. And when he finished with that he took off one of his arms. I thought to myself "My God! What IS this?" And he lay there on the bed, just his trunk and one arm with his erect cock! I remember thinking his cock made it look like he had two arms... one regular size and one little one.

Well, I feel bad about it even now, but it was just too much for me. I told him I couldn't do it, I was sorry but I just couldn't. He asked me why, and all I could say, over and over, was that I just couldn't. It was just too strange for me. "But I'm all exited, I want you" he told me. I kept repeating that I just couldn't, I was too nervous, I had to leave. He put $50 on the little table, which was a lot of money back then, and asked me PLEASE not to leave. But I just couldn't do it. He called out after me, "Muchacha! Muchacha! Please!" and I called back to him that I would get him another girl. So I went downstairs and saw Yvette. Yvette was a very nice person, a little older, but she wasn't all that good looking and didn't get all that many customers. So when I told her about the guy with no legs and just one arm, she said she would do it, and she went upstairs and took care of him. And even though she wasn't much to look at, he still gave her a really good tip. I would have probably made even more than she did because I could tell he really liked me, but I just couldn't do it.

The other girls saw me and I was white as a sheet. They asked me if I had done too much coke and I told them no. I told them about the gringo and how he took off his legs and an arm. I would later joke that I was afraid he would take off his cock too, but at the time I was just scared to death. It was the strangest thing that had ever happened to me, up to that point at least. I couldn't get it out of my mind. I couldn't work anymore that night and I kept thinking about it for weeks. It really bothered me. I was still very young, maybe seventeen or eighteen. Maybe now I would be able to handle it better. I think so. But back then it really upset me. I had nightmares about him for a long time.

FABI

I was doing pretty well at the El Jardin. I had no boyfriend or girlfriend to take care of me or tell me what to do, and I was earning money with the men there and selling a little drugs too, mostly to the girls there and sometimes the gringos. I was still young, maybe nineteen. I had lived a lot in my nineteen years, but in some ways I still had a lot to learn. It was around that time that Fabi got out of jail. I remember running into her for the first time after we were in jail together at the bar across from the El Jardin. She was with her girlfriend, Lali. They were together before Fabi went to jail, and got back together when she got out.

I had my first lesbian experience in jail with Fabi, who protected me from Maria Felix who was going to rape me with a broom handle. When we were in jail, we were girlfriends, but when she finally got out she went back to Lali. I know she liked me better than Lali, because Lali wasn't all that attractive. She was fat and not good looking. And of course I was definitely in my prime at the time. It wasn't any accident that I was the most popular girl in Hotel El Jardin.

I was still grateful to Fabi and still cared for her but when I would run into the two of them, I would usually try avoiding them or just leave. I didn't want any problems with Lali. Lali knew that Fabi and I had been together in jail, and she was the jealous type. She was a pretty rough person in her own right. Sometimes when Lali would go to the bathroom, Fabi would come over and talk to me, and I could tell she wanted to be with me, but she was with Lali and I didn't want to get in the middle of that. I had enough trouble in my life. I didn't have to go looking for it.

Lali was like a lot of the people I had known in my life, a small time criminal. She sold drugs and would steal when she could. Fabi wasn't any different, for that matter. I don't know how long they would have stayed together, but Lali got arrested again and went to jail. So when Fabi became "free," it wasn't long before she talked me into moving in with her in Paso Ancho. *[Paso Ancho is another barrio on the outskirts of San José, maybe a few miles north of Desamparados.]*

We didn't live together for all that long, maybe six months. I was doing alright as a prostitute and selling cocaine, but Fabi wanted me to quit working... she wanted to take care of me. I didn't hate working at Hotel El Jardin but I didn't totally love it either. There were good times and times that weren't so good. When Fabi offered to take care of me, it sounded better to me than what I was doing. I wouldn't have to work, except I would be the "wife" and take care of the house and my girls and Fabi. I didn't mind that at all. I'm a very neat and clean person, and cleaning is something I do for myself as much as anything else.

Fabi was a big woman, very macho, but the funny thing is that she had three children! She wasn't that old either, only three or four years older than I was. But she was married before she knew me, before she knew Lali, probably before she had been in jail or had been with a woman. So she had three children and I had my two and we all lived together in her place in Paso Ancho.

She supported us all selling cocaine and shoplifting, which she did along with some of her friends. One would distract the girl working in the shop while another would steal and take things to another person outside. She was a good provider and took very good care of me and my girls. She was always giving me jewelry, lots of gold bracelets, necklaces, things like that. It was something I had never had as a girl, somebody who gave me things and treated me tenderly. Osote wasn't all that bad to me, but Fabi treated me with more kindness, and she wasn't as wild and crazy as Osote.

Our relationship was pretty good, when I think back. We fought once in a while, as you might imagine. I was, and still am a flirt by nature. She would get jealous when other women or men paid attention to me. So once in a while we'd fight, but most of the time we were fine together. I wasn't in love with her, though I think she was in love with me. But I wasn't in love with Osote either, or Eduardo for that matter. I was fond of Fabi and Eduardo, and Osote too, more or less, but I wasn't in love with any of them. At that point in my life I had never really been in love.

GOODBYE TO FABI

Fabi and I lasted about a half a year, but I messed it up. Fabi had a good friend, Clara, who would come to our house sometimes to visit or do business. Clara was a lesbian, like most of our friends. One day when Fabi was out shoplifting, Clara came by. Well, I was horny and I knew Clara was attracted to me, so we started fooling around on the sofa and all of a sudden, Fabi came back and caught us kissing and partly undressed. Clara tried to hide by running into the bathroom, but Fabi took out her .22 pistol and BOOM, shot Clara in the foot. "You aren't my friend! That's MY WOMAN!" she shouted.

One of the neighbors, Olga, just happened to be right outside when this happened. She ran in and grabbed Fabi and tried to calm her down. I told her, "Olga! Get Fabi out of here. She's trying to kill Clara. When the police come, if they catch her with the pistol she'll go back to jail for sure!" So Olga was able to get Fabi away, and once they were gone I called a taxi and I took Clara to the hospital. Once I knew she was being taken care of and was going to be alright, I went back to the house. When I got there, Fabi had all her clothes in bags outside the house. She moved out and never came back. That was the end of our relationship.

I stayed in the house for a while after Fabi left, but eventually the girls and I moved back to Desamparados. I worked the next few years in Hotel El Jardin, and did a little drug sales just like I did before. I moved quite a few times. Sometimes I'd be back in Desamparados, sometimes I would be renting a cheap hotel room near my work. The girls were usually with me, but not always. I can't remember all the different places I stayed in the time between Fabi and the next serious relationship I would have.

CLARA

I didn't hear anything about Clara again for quite a while. But about two years later, Clara was murdered by her girlfriend. The girlfriend, whose name was Laura, had stabbed her with a kitchen knife. I have no idea why, other than Laura was crazy. After she murdered Clara, she put Clara's body behind the sofa and left the body there for three days while she carried on as if nothing was wrong, as if nothing had happened... watching television and eating in the same room where Clara's dead body was rotting behind the sofa. Three days in a room with a corpse, as if nothing had happened! It gives me chills when I think of it.

The neighbors eventually smelled the dead body and called the police, who came and took Laura to jail. But she didn't end up in the regular jail, but went to a sort of jail/hospital for crazy criminals. While she was in jail all she kept saying was "Clara, Clara! Come here!" over and over. I don't know if Laura is still alive or not.

GEORGE

I went back to the El Jardin after Fabi and I was back doing the same things... partying, working as a prostitute and selling some drugs. My memory is a little hazy, but it might have been a year or two after Fabi left that I met George. I think I was around twenty two at the time and I'd say he was around fifty, but very nice looking, very elegant. I was in Hotel El Jardin along with some other girls when three gringos came in, all very well dressed. The girls and I all got up to greet them and welcome them. One of the men called me over but I could see that one of his friends wanted me too. So I called over one of the other girls and went over to talk to the other guy, who said his name was George. I thought he was very nice looking, and very classy, the kind of man I really like.

We began talking and he asked me my name, how old I was and all that sort of small talk. He eventually asked me why I was working in a place like Hotel El Jardin. He said I was too young and pretty to work there. Didn't I want to do something else with my life? I told him yes, I would love to do something else but I never went to school and there weren't any jobs for girls without any education.

We must have spent two hours talking and drinking. He asked me all kinds of questions and I told him all about my life. Finally after about two hours he told me he wasn't going to have sex with me in Hotel El Jardin, and I was thinking "oh shit, I need the money!" He said he had to go because there was some sort of conference he had to attend back at his hotel. But he gave me his telephone number and told me to call him the next day and we'd see each other. He said he didn't want to be with me in Hotel El Jardin, but wanted me to come to his hotel. He told me I should go home and take care of my children. I told him I needed to work because I didn't have any money and no customers that day, that I had spent two hours talking to him and hadn't made anything. So he handed me $30, which was a ton of money back then for no sex. Then he handed me another $20 and said it was for my children, and asked if I would just go home. He told me I could trust him, and I was thinking, "Oh my God!"

I went back home, very happy. I stopped on the way and got some groceries and even some Chinese food, which was a luxury for us. And when I went to bed that night I kept thinking of him and all he had said and done. So I called him the next day and he said "Hello Magdalena, I'm so glad you called me, I've been thinking of you." I told him I had been thinking about him as well. He asked me if I could come visit him at his hotel. I told him yes, but was it far away? He told me it was the Hotel Cariari, and I gasped! It was a very rich hotel, very expensive. I told him I didn't know what bus to take to get there and I didn't have any money left because I had bought food and shoes for the baby. He said not to worry, he'd send a taxi for me.

He sent one of the taxi drivers from the hotel, and he also sent a very elegant dress for me to wear, something classy. Nothing I had would fit in at a hotel like that. The taxi driver said that George wanted me to put the dress on before we went to the hotel, so I did. I had never worn anything like that before, it was very expensive, I could tell. It felt like a dream, like Cinderella. He also had the taxi driver give me ten dollars to pay for a babysitter because he wanted to spend the whole night with me. So I gave the ten dollars to the babysitter, got in the taxi, and we drove off to the hotel.

When I got there George gave me a big hug and was very, very sweet to me, very loving. So we had dinner and spent the night together. The next day he took me shopping, He bought me blouses, dresses, tennis shoes, earrings, a necklace, so much stuff! He was a rich man, a millionaire at least.

We spent pretty much all week together. A day or two before he left he told me he didn't want me to go back to work as a prostitute, that he wanted me to stay in my house and take care of my babies and he would call me every day there, in my house. I asked him what house? I only had a tiny room for us. That's when he told me he wanted to buy me a house. I asked him if he knew how much a house cost, and he said no, but in Costa Rica (then) he was sure it would be pretty cheap. So he said let's go look and we went to a little project not too far from where my mother lived, some new houses... basic but new. He asked me if this was a house I wanted and I said I liked it, so he said let's go to the office and we went. He had them get the paperwork ready and when the time came he pulled out a giant roll of dollars, probably $5000 or more, and just bought the house for me! I told him no, it was too much. I was shaking. But he insisted and when it was all done I had my own house! I was so happy I was crying.

Then he took me to a furniture store and told me to get whatever I needed. I told him I couldn't believe it, that I felt like I would die. He told me just to do it, that he didn't have much time before he had to leave and he wanted to be sure I had what I needed. He bought me a bed and one for my daughters, and all the things I needed for the kitchen and the rest of the house. He bought me furniture for the living room, appliances, three beds, dressers, a stove, a refrigerator, a microwave, even two televisions. I can't even remember it all, it was so much.

When it was time for him to leave, we were both crying. He gave me $500 to live on until he came back, which was quite a lot of money in Costa Rica back then. Once I got my telephone installed he would call me twice a day, to make sure I was in the house and not back working in Hotel El Jardin. He checked up on me all the time. Twice a month he would send me another five hundred dollars. And when he came to visit, which was every six months or so for a few days or maybe a week, he would bring two bags full of clothes, one for me and one for my daughters.

I felt really lucky to have a house and all the other things, and to have real security in my life for myself and my girls. I was grateful to George for all he had done for me. I had almost everything I could have wanted but I was young and foolish. I never saved any of the money he was giving me. I spent it on partying with my friends, buying drugs and alcohol for everybody. All my friends knew I was getting all that money and they took advantage of me.

George didn't know what I was doing because when he would visit I would stop partying and I would spend all my time with him. But as soon as he left I went back to drinking and doing drugs and all that. I have no excuse except that was the life I knew, it was how I had almost always lived. When George was around it was easy for me to stay out of trouble. We enjoyed being together and we cared for each other. But most of the time he wasn't there. I always got bored. I would watch television and do housework, but when friends would come over with some mota or guaro I would just naturally join in.

As time passed, George came to Costa Rica less and less often, but he still sent me money and supported me and my girls. It was a lot more than I ever had, but I wasn't satisfied with that. George gave me security but that wasn't enough. I wanted fun and excitement. I was so stupid.

MIGUEL

George was still sending me money and calling me when I first met Miguel and his wife. They were working in a dance club I liked to go to. I guess they must have heard of me somehow and knew that I had worked as a prostitute because Miguel and his wife told me that they wanted to pay me to have sex with Miguel's younger brother, who was still a virgin. He was a nice looking boy and I like sex, plus they were going to pay me a little to do it, but at first I told them I didn't want to. They asked me if I was afraid and I told them no, I wasn't afraid. They said I must be scared or I would do it. So I said, well, okay, I'll prove I am not afraid, let's do it. So they introduced me to the little brother and took us to a little room behind the discotheque where we had sex.

I didn't see any of them again until maybe a half a year later when I went a different dance club in Zapote, and I saw them both there, working. She worked in the ticket booth and he was "security." He walked around keeping an eye on things in case there was trouble.

I thought Miguel was very good looking and I was attracted to him, even though he was married. While his wife was in taking tickets he would watch me dancing and we would smile at each other and more or less flirt. I didn't feel like I was betraying a friend because I barely knew his wife. If some handsome man wanted to flirt with me, that was fine. If I was sitting at a table and he walked by, we would make eyes at each other and so on. It became pretty obvious that we both wanted each other, so he told his wife he wanted her to stop working at the ticket booth. They fought about this, but in the end she gave up working there and stayed at home. When this happened, the flirtation between us got stronger and we ended up going to short term/hourly hotels to have sex. This went on for about two months, when finally he told his wife he was leaving her and he moved in with me into the house George had bought for me.

I probably should have felt guilty but I didn't give it much thought. George hadn't been around for a long time. He was still calling me pretty often but he almost never visited anymore. When Miguel moved in with me and the girls, I thought I would just have him go away when George decided to visit, but it turned out that George never visited again so that part wasn't a problem.

Miguel and I lived together and lived well on George's money for about a year. I suppose we could have gone on that way for a long time. All that money was great, but Miguel was jealous of George, even though George was thousands of miles away. George wasn't visiting me anymore, but he still called me a lot and Miguel didn't like it. We'd be partying in the house with some friends and George would call and everybody would have to shut up while we were on the phone. Miguel didn't like it, and he told me I would have to choose between them, either tell George goodbye or Miguel would leave me. I had to choose between Miguel and George.

I know it doesn't make sense now, but I was in love with Miguel and I didn't want to lose him, so I did what he asked me to do and broke off with George. When I told George I think he wanted to die, he seemed so heartbroken. He called one day and I broke the news to him that I had fallen in love with another man and it was over between us. I still feel really bad about hurting George that way when I think about it. He was so good to me and gave me so much. But what I wanted right then was right in front of me and I chose Miguel.

I feel so stupid now, giving in to Miguel, and I feel ashamed of what I made him do. Miguel and his wife had a son, and I told Miguel didn't want his son around, not even to visit. I did the same thing to him he did with me and George. I made him choose between me and his own son. I'm not proud of that. I can't explain it. I know now that it was wrong, and I feel bad about it when I think of it. I think it must have been my way of getting back at Miguel for making me give up George and everything George was still giving me... still giving US, really. If he was going to make me do something I didn't want to do, I was going to get back at him, and I did. Of course it didn't make things better.

Neither of us sat down and figured out what we were going to do for money now that George wasn't going to be sending me any. I can't even do arithmetic and I don't think Miguel was much better. I knew there was going to be less money coming in, that's all. At the time we were selling some drugs and we fooled ourselves into thinking that we'd be able to get by. I remember we would buy an ounce of cocaine with the idea we'd sell little amounts of it and turn a profit. What actually happened was we'd end up snorting up all the profits ourselves. Mostly we were just partying and living the high life. We weren't thinking about the future.

Some of my friends tried to tell me I was fucking up, but I didn't listen. The rest of our friends were partying with us and they didn't want the party to stop. And we didn't want to hear it anyway. We were just living for the moment, not thinking about the future. And we weren't in much condition to think even if we wanted to, with all the drugs and alcohol. I was still only twenty one or twenty two and just about everybody I knew just spent their money whenever they got some. Miguel and I did the same. Miguel didn't want me to work but he didn't want to work either. We would spend every day and night every night together.... having sex, drinking and doing cocaine. Our "friends" were happy to join us in the big party.

It's no surprise that we weren't bringing in enough to keep the party going forever. As we began to run low on cash, we started to pawn or sell some of the furniture or whatever. We did have some drug money coming in, so it happened slowly, over years.

LISETH

I met Liseth right around the time I met Miguel. George was still sending me money but he wasn't calling every day to check up on me, so I still had my house and I had my freedom too. I would still go to Hotel El Jardin just to party with my friends and I could go out at night whenever I wanted to. I was at a dance club one night when Liseth came up to me and told me that she wanted to meet me because girls she knew were talking a lot about me, how well I had done working at Hotel El Jardin and how I had met this rich gringo who was sending me money. At the time she was living with a guy who was very abusive. She wanted to get away from him. She told me that she would like to have a life like mine, and what did she need to do? She saw that I lived very well and was always going out partying and my life was carefree and I always had money.

I told her I could help her. We would start by changing the way she dressed, because she was dressing like an old married woman. She told me she was afraid that if she left the guy she was with, he would hunt her down and kill her. I told her she could come stay at my house, that I'd let her have a room until she found work or a gringo.

Back then she was as thin as I was and my clothes would fit her. At first I started to take her to Hotel El Jardin and she began working there as a prostitute. But one day she told me that she had to go visit her mother and when she came back she had a black eye, because she had run into her ex boyfriend. So I took her to the courthouse so she could file a complaint against the guy for assault, and after that we never heard any more from him.

From the very beginning she did well as a prostitute. She has a pretty face and back then had a nice body too. Soon she had enough money to rent a room of her own. She would come by my house so we could go to the El Jardin together. She went to work and I just went to party. We were close like that for about three months. But by the end of that time she knew how to fend for herself and didn't need my help any more. Once she had things going, we didn't see that much of each other, except when I went to party at Hotel El Jardin. She did come around once in a while to our house, but I noticed she was looking at Miguel a lot. I am a jealous person, and I asked her please not to visit me when Miguel was there. If she wanted to see me, okay, but I didn't like how she was looking at Miguel. After that she stopped coming over and we would only talk on the phone once in a while. I felt Liseth was pretty ungrateful at the time, but I wouldn't find out just how ungrateful until later.

AMALIA

Liseth wasn't the only girl I had a problem with. There was this young girl who lived close by, very, very pretty, with long blonde hair and a slim, sexy body. I would see her around the neighborhood and since I like women too, I found her quite attractive. Well, as I said, Miguel and I did a little drug dealing for extra cash, and the girl, Amalia, came over to buy some mota. For one reason or other, I went back into the bedroom for a minute and when I came out I saw the two of them suddenly hiding something in their hands and acting very suspiciously. I have a jealous nature and I just knew something was up and I got very angry and began shouting at Amalia and Miguel, accusing them of planning something behind my back. Amalia got scared and took off, so I only had Miguel to yell at. Eventually I calmed down but I told him I had better not catch them together or there would be big trouble. Amalia stopped coming around then, just like Liseth did. We didn't see or hear much about either one for a while.

Amalia wasn't even eighteen yet, and our son Alan wasn't born yet. After Miguel and I split up, years later, Miguel eventually ended up with Amalia for a while. She even had a daughter by him. But that's not the strangest part of the story. About ten years after Miguel and I split up I saw my son Alan in the car with an older woman. He was probably fifteen at the time. And guess who the older woman was? Amalia! Later that day when he came home I told him that I saw him in the car with Amalia. I wasn't angry or anything, I thought it was funny, more than anything else. He told me he had been seeing her off and on, and that they had been fucking just that afternoon! I had to laugh. Here was my young teenage son, fucking Amalia, his father's ex and his step-sister's mother. What a world!

PREGNANT AGAIN

After Miguel and I had been together for about a three years, I got pregnant. We were happy about it. We still had money to spend and we were still in love, even though we fought a lot. That didn't seem unusual to either of us. Almost everybody we knew fought with their lovers. Everything was going fine, we thought. We weren't looking ahead. Life was still one long party.

One night when I was about four months pregnant, Miguel and I decided to go out and to do a little business, sell some drugs, and have a little fun. I was showing a little bit but still my usual flirtatious self, and dressed pretty sexy. We went and sat in a booth in this bar we knew, having a couple of beers and doing a little business selling cocaine. I guess everybody knows that when you're pregnant you have to pee more often than usual, and we were drinking beer, so I told Miguel I needed to go and got up to go to the bathroom. I was wearing a short skirt, as always, but it was pleated, not tight, you know? Anyway, there were three guys sitting in the next booth. And on my way back from the bathroom one of them lifted up my skirt to try to see my panties. And just at that moment Miguel had stood up to give me room to get into the booth and he saw what the guy did.

In a heartbeat Miguel grabbed the guy and started punching him in the face, and in a matter of seconds the guy was bleeding. The other two guys sitting with him didn't do anything to stop Miguel, but one of the guys went over to the bar and started talking to some of their friends. I knew something was up. I told Miguel to watch out and he stopped hitting the guy. By now there were about a dozen guys at the bar coming towards Miguel, shouting, cursing, all that. Miguel shouted back he'd take any of them on, one on one, but they said more or less "fuck that" and they were all going to gang up and beat the shit out of him.

Well, there was something they didn't count on. Miguel had a .22 pistol and I always carried it in my purse because back then they didn't have police women and men weren't allowed to search a woman's purse. So I pulled out the .22 and fired it into the ceiling. BAM! BAM! BAM! Well, as you can imagine, that got the attention of the guys who thought they were going to beat up Miguel! They took off running out the door, along with everybody else in the place . Miguel and I didn't waste any time getting out of there either. I put the pistol back in my purse and we grabbed the first taxi we could find and hurried back home.

MORE LISETH

I was about two months along when I became aware that I was pregnant with Alan. Liseth was also pregnant by a guy who was the typical worthless Tico: no job, no money, and no intention of being a real father. She got pregnant a little before I did. One day in December she came to my house with the baby because she had been having problems with the guy she was living with. They had been living in a hotel and she told me that she didn't want to see him anymore but didn't know what to do. One more time I helped her out and told her she could stay with Miguel and me in our house. Although she had been ungrateful before, I felt sorry for her and told her she could stay with us.

She came over, but as usual, Miguel and I had been arguing. We had a Christmas tree in the house and Miguel pushed me against the tree and I stumbled. Liseth got between Miguel and me so Miguel wouldn't push me or hit me anymore. But she had just recently given birth, her wound opened and she was very afraid because Miguel was very aggressive and very fucked up on drugs. The next day she told me that it would be better if she went back to the hotel because Miguel scared her. I didn't try to stop her. Miguel and I weren't getting along very well and I didn't need somebody around to make me jealous.

My relationship with Miguel was getting worse and worse. Along with the fights, the drugs, the jealousy and the insecurity, we were running out of money. Neither of us was working other than some small time drug sales. We gave away more than we sold. The obvious thing to do would have been to cut back on the partying. But instead we decided to sell the house George bought for me. Most of the other things were gone by then, the furniture and jewelry George bought for me. We had pawned or sold that to keep the party going, so we sold the house and with the money we put a down payment on a new house in and a used car that Miguel planned to use to work as a pirate taxi and sell drugs on the side. By this time I had made up my mind that I was going to leave Miguel, but I wanted to do it in the way that I thought was best for me and the children, so I was patient. The new house was going to take six months to build, so in that time we rented a place in Desamparados (again) and Miguel had the car that he could drive as a pirate taxi to make some money. That was the plan.

Miguel didn't turn out to be interested in working as a pirate taxi driver, though. I wasn't all that surprised. I was smart enough to have both the new house and car put in my name. Those last months were bad. Miguel wasn't making anything with the taxi and the fights were worse than ever. I had already made a firm decision to leave. If I didn't, one of us was going to end up killing the other. See this scar? *[Shows scar about eight inches long on her forearm].* I got that right before I decided I had to leave forever. I'd been thinking about leaving him for a long time but I didn't know how I would be able to do it. Miguel was violent and I knew he wasn't just going to let me leave peacefully. And I needed someplace to go with my children. But after selling the house George bought for me, I eventually came up with a way to do it.

LEAVING MIGUEL

I timed leaving Miguel with when the house in Zapote was ready. I knew that Miguel wouldn't just let me move out without a fight, and that I might even end up dead, so I called the police and told them I wanted to leave Miguel but I was afraid that he would kill me. When they finally showed up, they stayed and made sure Miguel didn't do anything. I had hired a truck and a driver and I put my things in the truck, and the children and I moved to the new house in Zapote. I took the car with me and got a restraining order against him. He had to stay away or they would take him to jail. That was the end of my relationship with Miguel. I still had feelings for him. I loved him and hated him, but the relationship was over. I can't turn my feelings on or off like a light switch but we had to get out. It was for my own safety and for the children. My mother never cared what happened to me when I was a child but I wasn't going to put my children in danger that way. Even when Miguel and I were together, I never let him lay a hand on any of my children.

When I left I took the car too, because it was in my name. It was a stick shift, and I had a friend help me find somebody with an automatic to trade for it. There was still a little bit of money left over from the house sale, so I wasn't in a panic. But my plan was to go back to working at Hotel El Jardin.

ZAPOTE

Zapote is a better place than Desamparados. It is safer, the houses are nicer and there isn't as much crime. It was good to be away from the bad influences but we were also away from family and people we knew. It was never difficult to find a babysitter in Desamparados but when we first got to Zapote I didn't know anyone locally except the owner of the "pulperia" [small neighborhood grocery store]. Now that I was rid of Miguel I wanted to enjoy my freedom and go out partying again. I asked the woman in the pulperia if she knew anybody to baby-sit and she said there was a young couple who lived in a room next to the pulperia and they might be interested. So I went over and knocked on the door. I asked them if they were interested in babysitting and they said "sure."

I had them come over about six that evening. I was dressed and ready to go. My kids were used to babysitters so after I explained where the food was for the kids, I left to go dancing and drinking. I don't remember what I did that night, where I went or who I saw, but I remember finally coming home late the next afternoon and opening the door to find that the babysitters had robbed me. They took my clothes my jewelry and whatever they could carry off. They had spent the night with the children, then, when the children went out to play the next day, they took all they could carry and left. When I finally got home, all I remember is how angry I was at the babysitters and how hung over I felt from the alcohol and cocaine I had done the night before. Things were not beginning well for me in Zapote. I finally found a couple of reliable babysitters through Liseth. That was the last thing she ever did FOR me. It wasn't the LAST thing she did TO me, though.

There were two famous singers who were going to do a concert in Costa Rica: Eros Ramazotti and Gloria Trevi. I had already decided to go when one of the other girls from the El Jardin, Patricia, told me she was going, and that she heard that Miguel and his brother were going too. I didn't expect to run into him so I didn't think much about it. I went with my friend Evelyn and Patricia went with Liseth. The concert was good and I enjoyed myself. I didn't see Patricia, Liseth, Miguel or his brother there and that was fine with me. My feelings toward Miguel at that time were a strong combination of love and hate. Even though I had separated from him I wasn't totally "over" him. I made a decision that we couldn't live together, but it hurt.

It was about a week later that Patricia got into some sort of argument with Liseth. I suppose it was for revenge that Patricia decided to tell me what happened after the concert. She told me that Liseth had paid her to have sex with Miguel's brother and Liseth had paid Miguel to have sex with her! Paid him! They went to an hourly hotel and Liseth paid for it all, which cost quite a bit.

When I heard this I felt like I wanted to die. I had done so much for Liseth for years and years. Miguel and I had separated several times before and gotten back together. Liseth couldn't have known that we had split up forever. Nobody could have. But Liseth took the first chance she got to move in on Miguel. She even PAID for it all! I realized that I was right all along to suspect her of wanting Miguel even when Miguel and I were together. I did so much for her and all the while she was after my boyfriend. That did it with for me with Liseth. I have never spoken to her again. She knew very well that if I had wanted to do it I could have beaten the shit out of her but I preferred to just let things be. Liseth tried to make up with me many times but I can't forgive her. I don't hate her any more but I don't want that kind of person in my life.

I went back to working the El Jardin and I had plenty of customers. I was still in my prime, in my late twenties. But even though I was making money, I was falling behind on the payments for the car and the house. Instead of making sure I had enough to make the payments, I was out late every night spending whatever I had earned on the same old things, living like tomorrow would never come. I spent way too much on alcohol and cocaine. By the time we moved to Zapote and the new house, I hardly had any money left from selling the house George had bought for me. We sold it too cheaply, for one thing. The only excuse I have is that I was young and stupid. By the time the children and I got to Zapote, and after the babysitters took what they could carry, I didn't have much left.

I was falling behind on the house and car payments, but I took care of the car problem by crashing it. I was out drinking one night and ran it into a cement pillar of an overpass. I just left the car there and took a taxi home. I had already pretty much stopped making payments anyway. I called the police the next day and reported it stolen. I never heard any more about it.

But I was getting calls about being behind in the house payments, and I was having trouble paying water bills and light bills and everything. I didn't like all those responsibilities and I wasn't good about paying bills. For me it was very difficult because I never went to school long enough to learn to add or subtract even. I taught myself to read and write, but I'm not good at it. And all the drugs, alcohol and late nights didn't help either. It got to be overwhelming for me.

I finally decided that I wanted out from owning a house, so I decided to sell it. There was a little equity left from the down payment and after it was sold, the children and I moved to an apartment in San Sebastian. I was still working at Hotel El Jardin, and the apartment was cheaper than the house, plus the water and electricity were included in the rent. So life was easier for me.

I have to admit I didn't spend a lot of time with my children. I wasn't as bad as my own mother. None of my children ever went hungry or went without decent clothes to wear. They all went to school as long as they wanted to. But I didn't spend much time with them or pay a lot of attention to them. Maybe if I had spent more time with them and given them more attention, they would have turned out differently. It would have made a lot of difference to me, I think, if my mother had been a real mother and not an alcoholic and if I had some sort of education and not grown up around all the drugs and violence. But the past can't be changed.

Valeria was thirteen by then, Gloriana was eight and Alan four. Valeria had grown up to be a serious girl and I began to have her watch the other children when I went out to work and party. The El Jardin was my main place, as it had been before I was with Miguel and during our time together. Alex, one of the owners at the time, was glad to have me back working again. He always said if he had four girls just like me, he could retire in a year. Alex is a sweet man.

TRIP TO CANADA

I had been back working at the El Jardin for only a few months when I met this Canadian guy, Charles, who told me he was in love with me. After about a year of knowing each other, he asked me to come visit him in Canada. I had never been out of Costa Rica before, and he was going to pay for everything along with paying me for being with him. Charles was a heavy drinker and I wasn't in love with him, but he wasn't a bad guy, so I thought why not? We were planning on two weeks, so I made sure the rent was paid and there was food in the house. Valeria was fourteen now and old enough to watch the other two, but I asked Pati to check on them every day and I left money with her too.

Charles bought me a round trip ticket and back then there was no problem about needing a visa. So I flew from San José to Ottawa. The trip took about twelve hours, and I was very tired when I got there. I went through immigration and customs, and I was expecting Charles to be waiting there for me, but I didn't see him near the exit. I stood there waiting for at least a half hour, but Charles never showed up. I decided to walk around the terminal and look for him but he was nowhere around. I have never felt so lost in my life. It seemed like most of the people around me were speaking French, and I only knew a tiny bit of English. Nobody spoke Spanish. I spent eight hours in the airport, just praying that Charles would show up any minute. I was so stressed out. I didn't even have any money with me. I just had the return ticket. I was so hungry and tired I wanted to die. When Charles finally showed up, he told me there had been a freak snowstorm and he couldn't get to the airport. He was stuck in traffic, I guess, and this was before cell phones, so he couldn't get a message to me. I was so relieved when I finally saw him that I forgot right away how terrible it had been.

Charles had a LOT of money, and because it was so cold and snowy, he just went to the counter and bought us two tickets to Puerto Vallarta in Mexico. So all I got to see of Canada was the Ottawa airport before we were off to Mexico. I felt a lot more comfortable when we got to Mexico. Everybody spoke my language and Charles got us a nice room in a very nice hotel right near the beach. I got a little sleep on the airplane but I was very tired and as soon as I had showered I lay down on the bed and fell asleep.

Ever since I began working at Hotel El Jardin, I was used to staying up late and sleeping late. Any night that I got to sleep before three in the morning was an early night for me. That wasn't Charles' schedule. He would get up pretty early in the morning, much too early for me. By the time I woke up around eleven or noon, Charles had been up several hours and since he was an alcoholic, he was already half drunk.

We got along pretty well, he wasn't a mean drunk, but he was still a drunk. I didn't mind drinking myself, and by mid afternoon we were both in a decent mood and usually had sex. After that we would go down to the bar and he would continue drinking, getting more and more drunk. He was like a lot of drunks and the more drunk he got, the more he liked to talk. My English wasn't very good then, and he had more to talk about with the other gringos at the bar. As for me, I watched the telenovelas on the television set in the bar or talked with Mexican guests or the bartenders and waitresses.

We would hang out in the bar all afternoon, or I would go lie around the swimming pool. When the Sun went down it was time to have dinner, and we would eat together. After we were done, he would order a bottle of whiskey and we would return to the room. By that time he was very drunk and I just watched television until he passed out.

I spent the first night just watching television until I got sleepy a LOT later, but when the same thing happened the next night, I decided to go back down to the bar and hang out. That's where I ran into some taxi drivers and we became friends. One of them had a little house up in the hills above Puerto Vallarta, and when the bar got boring we decided to go up to his house and continue the party. He had some mota and I liked mota, so off we went.

We only stopped at his house for a minute, just long enough for him to get a few things. I can't remember his name but he was nice looking, a little like Miguel only darker skin. There had been one other guy with us, but he got out along the road somewhere and it was just the one taxi driver and me. We drove up to a spot where you could look down at the lights of Puerto Vallarta and the ocean. He had a bottle of tequila and some mota so we did a little of each. It was very pretty and romantic, though I don't need romantic scenery to be horny.

We only smoked a little of the mota and had one shot of tequila before I had his pants unzipped and was giving him head. I don't really remember too much after that other than I know we had sex and I liked it. After that, he drove me back to the hotel. He was at the hotel bar the next night too, with a couple of friends, and we all went out together to a couple of discos they liked. He told me he'd be at the hotel the next night if I wanted to hang out with him and his friends. I didn't have anything better to do, so we went to a couple of bars/discos he liked. It's a little blurry in my memory, but I think we did that about three times before it was time to go back to Canada with Charles.

When we flew back to Canada, he wanted me to meet his mother. I guess he had ideas that we were going to get married or something. He may have told me but he was always drunk and I didn't take him all that seriously. But I met his mother, who was just an older lady I could barely talk to. She seemed nice enough but I really didn't get to know her.

I didn't like Canada because it was just too cold for me. It was nice, clean, modern and everything, but just too cold. But while I was there, I decided to get a tattoo. Stupid me, I thought because it was in a rich country like Canada it wouldn't hurt. I can sure be an idiot sometimes!

We were both out drinking beer somewhere in Ottawa and we both got good and drunk. I told him I wanted to get a tattoo. He said I was drunk. I told him that HE was drunker than I was, and I wanted to get a tattoo. He said he knew where we could go, and so we went to the place where I got a tattoo of a jaguar on my butt. I was pretty drunk and they used something to make the pain less. So while I was getting the tattoo it didn't hurt all that much. But the stuff they used to dull the pain wore off about the time the beer was wearing off, and the tattoo began to hurt really badly. I was hung over too, to make things even worse, and I was going crazy with the pain. I tried to scratch off the tattoo, as if that was going to work! It only made it worse, of course. How stupid could I get?

So with the tattoo bothering me and the weather and missing my children and my country, I told him I wanted to go back to Costa Rica. He had the airline change the date on my return ticket and I went back alone. He was angry with me but I was tired of him. He was always drunk, a slob. So that was the end of it with him, I never saw him again. I have no idea what happened to him.

Back from Canada

I was gone about two weeks and when I got back home I went back to working the El Jardin. It was just a coincidence that I had some money left from Charles and a friend told me about some lots they had for sale very cheap. Although I had told myself I didn't want to own a house, the lot was inexpensive and the owners would take payments, plus the government had a program to provide the material cheap for me to build a house, so I saved up enough to pay the down payment on a lot and pay for my part of the materials.

At first I hired three local guys to do the work but I wasn't happy with the work they were doing. I told a friend about it and she said I should talk to David. She said I might even be able to trade sex for work! Well, I had known him for years and although he was younger, that didn't bother me. So I got him working on the construction and we started having sex and pretty soon we were a couple and the sex and construction work were free.

He put up the outer walls first. One of my long time clients from Hotel El Jardin paid for the roof. Then David put in the bathroom and kitchen stuff and we moved in. There were no inside walls, but we divided it off with some bed sheets and I had a room, the kids had a room and we had a kitchen and bathroom.

I kept working at the El Jardin, but David and I stayed together after the house was done, though he never moved in with us. He was living close by with his mother and we saw each other often enough.

Up until I met David, I never did "piedra" ["rock" or "crack" cocaine] but he was doing it and when I gave it a try, I liked it. I still do it, but not very much, just once a day maybe, and it only lasts a short time. I can go without it but I like it.

While I was busy with David, the house, and Hotel El Jardin, Valeria was discovering boys. I knew she was growing up and I knew she had already had her first period. I also noticed that there were some boys who came in and out of the house. It seemed natural enough and I was busy with working at night and spending time with David so I really wasn't paying that much attention.

Valeria was always a little on the big side, and it took a while before I noticed that she was putting on weight, but it was just her belly. I suspected she might be pregnant even before that because she was getting sick, nauseous. I asked her if she was pregnant, and she told me no, But eventually there was no denying it and we had a big fight over it. She wasn't even fifteen yet. I asked her who the father was. It was a neighbor kid, not even anybody she was serious about. I didn't mind that she was having sex, but she could have used the pill or something. It was like she didn't even think about it.

Things calmed down and I eventually accepted the situation. The "father" didn't stay around, which is typical. Valeria didn't care. So she was just like me, pregnant at fourteen. Part of the reason I was angry is that her situation wasn't like mine. She didn't have a "Juan" to chase her out of the house and she had some education. Although she quit at thirteen at the end of grade six. That was six more years than I ever had. She didn't grow up hungry and in fear like I did. But she went and got pregnant anyway.

Things calmed down and went back to normal, more or less. The father of Valeria's baby didn't want to be a father, and all we heard was that he went off to Guanacaste somewhere to work. Valeria didn't care. The boy wasn't even really a boyfriend.

While she was pregnant she started seeing an "older" man, which meant a guy in his twenties in her case. It is the custom in Costa Rica to throw a big party for a girl's fifteenth birthday, called a "quinceñera." I told her that we'd have a party for her birthday alright, but we'd make it a baby shower. By then the new house was finished and we had all moved in.

Valeria didn't stay too long after the baby was born, though. She moved in with the "older" guy she had been seeing, who wanted to take care of her and her new daughter, Graciela. That was fine with me. Valeria and I didn't get along very well.

It was a little after Valeria left that something really scary and strange happened. I was in the house with Alan and the dog his father gave him. Alan was six or seven at the time. The dog was big like a wolf. Gloriana wasn't there. Maybe she was playing with her friends, I don't remember. But anyway, Alan and I were lying on the bed watching television when we heard a car go by twice. I thought it was kind of strange. The third time it passed, I heard the car stop and I heard somebody coming to the door. I told Alan to go open the door. I thought it was his father coming to leave Alan some money or something. So he opened the door and I heard some noise which turned out to be from the guy kicking Alan into a table. I got up and ran into the room where the guy and Alan were, and Alan was just getting up. The guy told me to keep quiet and do what he said. Then he grabbed Alan and put the gun to his head!

Well, I go crazy when there's danger and instead of being scared I got angry. I was actually getting ready to attack him when we all heard something outside, some noise. I could tell the guy was a Colombian by his accent, and I could also tell that he was nervous and unsure of himself. When we heard the noise I told Alan "There's your father coming home!" I am still amazed that I was thinking so quickly. But like I said, the Colombian wasn't sure of what he was doing, and he let go of Alan, put the pistol inside his pants and ran out the door. As soon as he was out the door I rushed over and locked it, then pushed a chair against it in case he tried to return, but he never did. And all this time the dog, this big dog that was supposed to be part wolf, did nothing at all. Nothing! If that dog was part wolf, a bigger part was chicken. What a pussy! .

I still don't know exactly why the Colombian broke in on us that day, or what he wanted. I thought I knew for a while. My ex-girlfriend from years before, Fabi, came over for to see the new house, and she had a very jealous girlfriend. I thought that the girlfriend might have set it up to scare me or something. But a few years later I was in Los Condes, a bar downtown, when I ran into the ex girlfriend of a lesbian I knew named Cindy. She told me that Cindy had set it up. I still couldn't figure it out until it occurred to me that I had a fair amount of cocaine in the house and they probably thought I had money there too. About all I can figure out is that it must have to steal the drugs and money. I barely knew Cindy then. That would change later on, but I barely knew her then.

David

Valeria had moved out a little while after Graciela was born and lived with an older man, but they were fighting and so eventually Valeria and Graciela moved back in with me. The house began to seem crowded and it seemed like somebody was always arguing with somebody else. Valeria was working by this time and I was tired of all the noise and I was spending a lot of time with David at his mother's house, so Valeria and I came to an agreement that she would take over paying the bills on the house and it would be hers and Gloriana's. They would take care of Alan and I would move in with David and his mother. The bills didn't amount to much, just a little payment on the lot and utilities. But I should have known she wouldn't pay the bills, and after about three months I told her no more and that I was going to sell the house for what I could. Miguel agreed to take Alan, Gloriana moved with my mother and Valeria and Graciela moved back in with the boyfriend.

I moved in with David because I was already spending a lot of time there and I was tired of all the fighting in the house. I wasn't ever really in love David, though I did feel attraction, especially at first. I moved in with him mostly because I was tired of the children fighting with each other and Valeria fighting with me. Not only that, but I didn't have to work and there was always crack and beer there.

There were four of us there. David and I lived in a little sort of house in back of the main house where the mother and his older brother, Juan lived. Everybody in the house worked except me, but I did the housework so nobody complained about me. I didn't mind at all, I am naturally a very clean and tidy person. David's mother worked as a housecleaner when she could and Juan worked construction like David. Sometimes they worked together and sometimes they didn't. .

I didn't go to Hotel El Jardin while I was living with David and his family. I didn't go there to work and I didn't even go there to party. I didn't really keep in contact with my old friends or even with my family. I saw them maybe three or four times in the two years I was with David. It was like a vacation from my life. I did the housework, of course. But I didn't go out to party. David always had crack for me and his mother always had beer. I like to watch television, so when I wasn't doing housework I would watch television while David was working. It wasn't too exciting, but it wasn't bad.

Things started out okay, but the longer I was there; the more I began to think about leaving. I was getting tired of the same old thing all the time, but it was David's brother, Juan, that finally made me decide to leave.

I always thought he was a little strange, that there was something wrong about him, but I couldn't say what it was. I was used to strange from working at Hotel El Jardin, and I had lived with Juan and my mother, so at first I wasn't really bothered when David's brother saw me one time in my bra and panties and told me he would pay me if I would walk around the house that way when his mother and David weren't around. I thought it was a little weird, but it seemed harmless and money was money.

Juan never tried anything with me and never asked me to have sex with him, but what happened was much worse. Everybody in the house would drink. David and I drank but not like his mother and Juan. His mother would drink until she passed out. Juan would drink too, but he just got weird and crazy.

What finally drove me out of the house was one night after David went to bed when I caught Juan trying to rape his mother, who had passed out. His mother had no idea what was going on, she was so drunk, but I ran over and started hitting him and yelling at him. He was drunk too, but I guess he didn't expect anybody to see what was trying to do, and he just mumbled and went into his room. I stayed up to make sure he didn't try it again, but he passed out himself and I locked his mother's door and tried to fall asleep on the sofa near the door to the mother's room. It was a very bad night.

I had been thinking about leaving before because I was bored, but seeing Juan trying to rape his own mother while she was passed out was too much. I decided that night that I would get out as soon as I could the next day after David left for work. He got up early and as soon as he left to go to work I started packing. I didn't have a whole lot, just clothes and some make up, things like that, and it all fit into the bag I had plus a couple of plastic bags I got from the kitchen. I called up a friend of mine who drove a pirate taxi and he came and got me. I had a little money saved up, enough to pay the taxi and pay for a few nights in a hotel. I never saw David or his mother and brother again. And that was the end of my "vacation."

THE CUBAN ADVENTURE

I went back to work at Hotel El Jardin, and it was great to see a lot of my friends. The boss was glad to see me because we liked each other and I brought in lots of customers when I was there before. I felt happy to be back and I felt welcome there.

It had been a couple of years and there were some new customers and some new girls but it felt about the same. There were still some of the same girls I had known for years. I wasn't a teenager any more, but I was still just past thirty and I had lots of customers. Lots of the newer guys had never seen me before, so they all wanted to go with me and I liked the money and I enjoyed the popularity, just like before.

I hadn't been back at the El Jardin for very long, maybe a few months, when a gringo came to the hotel looking for someone willing to go Cuba to get married with a man who wanted residency in Costa Rica. He said he would pay $2500. There were about eight girls there, and they all told him no. But I guess I was just braver or stupider than the rest because I told the gringo "yes," I would do it.

He asked me for my ID because he needed it to get me a passport, so I gave it to him and in about two weeks he back with the passport and a ticket so I could go for a week. I was afraid because I didn't know anybody in Cuba and I had to travel alone, but $2500 was a lot back then, so I went.

I arrived at the airport in Havana with a paper tucked into my bra with the name of the Cuban written on it. When I got off the plane, a man came up to me and said "Seniorita, you must be Magdalena" and I said yes, I was. He told me his name was "Lino." He was a nice looking man, and he took me to his house, where he was living with his girlfriend. I could tell the girlfriend was jealous, which I thought was silly because this whole marriage agreement was just business.

But she must have sensed something, because in the week that I was there, I fell in love with Lino and he fell in love with me, or at least that's how it felt at the time. But it was the arrangement that we would get married, and we did. While I was waiting to fly home, we would sneak away from the girlfriend and have sex. And on the last day before I left to return to Costa Rica, we all went out and I got very drunk and I got very jealous and got in a fight with the Cuban girlfriend over my husband. Now he was my husband, I felt in the right. He didn't know what to do with me so he sent me to spend the last night with a woman friend of his.

I came back to San José and went back to work at Hotel El Jardin. After I was paid, I didn't hear any more of my "husband" for a long time, well over a year. Then one night the bar was having its weekly "lesbian" show, and I was on the bar with a couple of the other girls, more or less having or pretending to have sex with them, when my Cuban "husband" came in. After two years not hearing anything of him, there he was. He said "Hello, my wife" and I wanted to die of shame. I jumped down from the bar and ran back to put on my clothes. When I got back, he had left. I never saw him again.

SKIP

There was one guy who used to come in to the Hotel named "Skip." Skip would take four or five girls up to his room at a time. He would always have a big bag of cocaine and he would insist that we all do lines with him. If we said "no" he would get angry and make us leave, so even the girls who didn't like cocaine much would do it because it was easy money. I liked cocaine, though as much as he did, so I was part of the group most of the time. He paid well too, so we'd party with him and get crazy. It's like he was trying to do everything all at once with the drugs and the girls. He had a big collection of sex toys and always wanted to try something new. I remember one time when I was alone with him he told me he had a fantasy. I asked him what his fantasy was. He told me it was to have a man give him a blow job while I watched. I was a little surprised but he paid well enough, so I said fine.

He told me to wait in the room and left for maybe ten or fifteen minutes. When he came back, he had a transvestite with him. Back then, the transvestites used to work back behind the church near Parque Central (Central Park), which was not far from the hotel. So he brought this transvestite back to his room and had me sit on the sofa and watch while the transvestite sucked him. I must have had a really strange look on my face because I know that I felt very strange. When Skip looked at my face and my expression, he suddenly seemed to get afraid or ashamed. "Stop!" he told the transvestite, and gave him some money to go away. He apologized for scaring me and told me that I gave better head than the transvestite!

He was there a lot and most of us got to know him pretty well. He had a wife in Guanacaste all the while he was coming up to San José to party with us. One time he came into the hotel very agitated. He told us that his wife had been in an airplane crash and had survived! And sure enough, it was on the news that night. I got the feeling he wished she had died. But eventually he stopped showing up, just like John the cat killer.

A lot of guys seem to like more than one girl at a time, though I don't see how it's worth it. After all, a man only has one penis, right? But most of the time when I've been with a guy and other girls it's usually more about partying than just sex. Of course there was sex too. A guy would have one girl sitting on his face, another on top of him and another kissing his nipples and he would be stroking another girl's breasts or something like that. With Skip, at least, when he wanted to finish, he would almost always just keep one or maybe two of his favorites there so he could concentrate. It's especially hard for guys who are doing cocaine to finish. It takes a lot of concentration or something.

It was easy work when there were a lot of us in the room with him. I mean, he only has one penis and one mouth. So maybe we would lick his nipples or maybe he would stroke our bodies but in general we didn't have to work too hard. Sometimes he'd want us to do each other. I never minded getting licked but I didn't like licking other girls. If the girl was clean and pretty and I was getting paid enough I'd be into it, but most of the time I was the one getting licked, not the one doing the licking.

The last time I saw Skip it was downtown, at least ten years later, and he had calmed down a lot. He wasn't doing drugs anymore. He told me he had had a couple of heart attacks and had to be careful now. But I think he had more than his share of fun. He probably did more in just the time I knew him than most men do all their life.

NORA

It was during the time when Skip was coming into the El Jardin when I went there one afternoon to work. As I walked in, I noticed a nice looking butch lesbian sitting at the bar. Ever since Fabi, I found myself attracted to butch looking women, though I still liked men too. But this butch had a classy look and I wondered what in the world she was doing in Hotel El Jardin.

So as I sat at one of the tables drinking a beer, I was watching this girl out of the corner of my eye. Another girl who worked there, Melissa, came down from upstairs where she had been with a client, and she sat at the table with me. She noticed how I was looking at the butch and asked me if I liked her (the butch). I said yes, she looked good to me. Melissa said the butch was a friend of hers called "Nora" and she would introduce us if I wanted her to. I said yes, that would be great.

So Melissa went over and spoke a few words to Nora, and they both came over to the table. Melissa introduced us and we talked together for about a half an hour. I found out that Nora had just been kicked out by her girlfriend, without much more than what she was wearing. Melissa had told Nora that maybe she could make some money at Hotel El Jardin. Nora was hoping to get enough money together to buy a little cocaine and divide it up into little lines to sell and make some money that way.

While we were talking together, Skip walked in. As usual, Skip was looking for a little party, and he asked Melissa if she and Nora would go upstairs to a room with him and put on a little lesbian show. He could see that Nora was obviously a lesbian. Melissa didn't hesitate and said yes, so Skip went over to pay for the room and Melissa told Nora what Skip wanted. Nora was hesitant but she needed some money and Melissa persuaded her to go upstairs with her and Skip.

When they got upstairs, Skip wanted Melissa and Nora to take off their clothes, but Nora was too shy. Skip seemed to understand, and he told her she could keep her clothes on, but he wanted to see her lick Melissa's pussy. Melissa lay down on the bed and spread her legs, but Nora just couldn't do it in front of Skip. Skip was nice about it, and told Nora it was okay, she could leave, which she did right away.

So she came down, sat with me, and told me what had happened upstairs. Well, I was doing okay at the El Jardin in that time, so I offered to loan her a little money so she could get started with her drug dealing business. She was very grateful to me, and promised to pay me back just as soon as she could. She gave me a big hug and I really liked it! Then she left to go see about getting her "merchandise." I didn't see her for about a week or so, but she came back to the El Jardin and gave me back what I loaned her, and thanked me again for helping her out. She said that she was back together with her girlfriend again and that things were okay between them. Well, I was a little disappointed because I was interested in her. Still, there was nothing I could do about it so I wasn't going to let it bother me.

But it wasn't too much later that Nora split up with her girlfriend for good. This time it wasn't like before, because the girlfriend didn't throw her out after a fight; they both just decided to end it. They divided up their furniture and things and the girlfriend left while Nora stayed in the house. Nora knew some of the dance places I liked to go when I wasn't working, and we started to see each other there. I was attracted to her and she was attracted to me, and it wasn't long before I moved in with her. We were attracted to each other physically but we were both somewhat famous back then. I was doing dance competitions and she was a drug dealer, and in a place like Leon XIII, a very bad neighborhood, she was an important person. So I think we both felt it was a good match.

After I moved in with Nora, I stopped working at Hotel El Jardin one more time. We were together for about six years. She was a very good businesswoman. She was very smart and well organized, and very good about money. When I met her that first day, she was just trying to put together a little money to buy some cocaine to divide into lines and resell. But she got to know dealers higher up in the business and she started buying and selling bigger and bigger quantities and making more money. She took care of me. But I never got involved in her drug business, I stayed out of it.

She was able to save up enough to open up a little bar in the center of San José and I worked there as a bartender. I liked that because I could keep an eye on her. I am always jealous when I'm in love with someone. I am always afraid they are going to leave me for somebody new. So I was working as a bartender and she was mostly involved in selling drugs there. She didn't sell directly much. She had other people selling them for her. This went on almost every day and we made good money.

But there were always problems, we didn't get along as well as Fabi and I did. We were both jealous persons and in a bar like that, there were always lots of people around and lots of flirting going on. Nora was getting more attention because she was becoming more successful. Towards the end she was selling kilos. We ended up with a really nice house in Tres Rios. It even had a Jacuzzi.

Drugs and alcohol were a problem. Nora didn't do drugs or drink, but I did enough for both of us. It was a very stressful life with a lot going on every day and a lot of drama. There were robberies, fights, drugs and alcohol and we always knew that the police might catch us doing something and put us in jail. She paid off some police to leave us alone but you never knew when things might change.

One fight we had was when my little brother Rodrigo got into a fight outside the bar and came in, bleeding. He had become a street person by then, a crack addict, and he hung out in front of the bar, causing problems sometimes. Anyway, when he came in he had been stabbed and was bleeding. He wanted me to help him but Nora told him he had to get out. So he left but we fought about it. Rodrigo was a bum, but he was my brother and he was bleeding.

That was just one time that we fought and I left, and went back to Hotel El Jardin. This happened maybe a few times every year. We would get into a fight, I would leave, maybe for a week, maybe for just a few days, then I'd come back again.

In the end, it was my jealousy and Nora's unfaithfulness that finally broke us apart. We had fought a lot and there was this one girl who I saw trying to give Nora her phone number secretly. I got angry but Nora told me that it was her niece. Well, I found out it was NOT her niece, and she was fooling around behind my back, so I left Nora and that bar and went back to Hotel El Jardin one more time.

I don't know if we would have gotten back together or not, because I was still in love with her, but while she was with the girl who wasn't her niece, they both got arrested for drug sales and went to jail. That was the end of my relationship with Nora. I have seen her recently and we were friendly, but that's all.

So I went back to working at Hotel El Jardin. I moved in with Fernanda, another woman who was working there. I was almost thirty then and Fernanda was probably around thirty-five. Fernanda lived with her lover, Andrea, and I had my two daughters with me, Valeria, her daughter Graciela and Gloriana. Valeria was maybe seventeen at the time and Gloriana was about eleven. We all lived together for about three months before there was a problem. Fernanda and I would go to work and leave Valeria and Andrea together. Well, Andrea seduced Valeria and Fernanda found out about it. So she kicked us all out in the street.

LEE SUTTON

One afternoon I went to work as usual. It wasn't very busy, just three girls there and one man. I said that it sure was quiet and the other girls said yes. Then a thin, good-looking and rather young gringo came in. I didn't pay him much attention because I preferred older men. The young ones were usually just there for a quick fuck and they didn't pay very well.

The other girls went over to him, one at a time, and asked him if he wanted company, and he said "no." But I thought I might as well give him a try, so I went over and sat down at the booth where he was sitting. I said hello to him and he said "Hello, you're very pretty."

I said "Thank you, but you don't want company?"

"Maybe," he said.

"But my friends said you didn't want company."

"Right, but they weren't as interesting as you," and he invited me to sit down next to him. So we had a couple of drinks and a guy came in selling flowers and he bought me flowers. After that he asked me if I'd go with him to the Nuevo Johnson Hotel where, he was staying. So we went there and had sex.

Afterward we were done; he asked me if I used any type of drug. I said yes, but I was embarrassed to tell him. He laughed and said if I told him what I used, he'd tell me what he used. So I told him I liked mota and sometimes I did cocaine. He said he did too, and asked me if I could get him some. I said sure. So he gave me some money and I went off and bought some cocaine.

We each did a couple of lines and I excused myself to go into the bathroom to smoke some of the "rock" [crack] I had also bought. I hadn't told him about that because people look down on it. When I came out there must have been a little smoke drift into the room because he asked me what the smell was. Since he smelled it, I told him. He said it smelled good. I told him how I made it. So he asked me to cook up some for him. I always carried around a little baking soda, and we already had the cocaine. You just add water and baking soda, dry it out and you get "rock."

He smoked some and obviously liked it. He had me go get some beer and some more cocaine and we started to party, nice and calm to start with. We went on for a while and I got to the point where I had had enough. I didn't want any more. But Lee kept wanting more, more, and more. I did it a little every day, and it was a habit, but I didn't let it get out of hand. I had a limit to how much I would do. Lee didn't have that limit.

We continued to see each other. I would go to his hotel and bring cocaine and I'd cook it for him and I'd have a little and he would have a lot. We went on that way every day for about three weeks. And by the end of the first two weeks, we were in love with each other. He told me he didn't want me to work any more as a prostitute. He asked me if I didn't want to stop working as a prostitute and I told him sure, but he was young, my own age, and he could find a girl who wasn't a prostitute. He told me I was very pretty and very sweet, and he asked me why I was doing this for a living, so I told him all about my life, how it was for me as a little girl, about Juan, about not going to school... everything.

I could tell that he felt sad hearing my story, felt sorry for how my life had been. So he told me that he wanted to try to have a relationship with me. So he took me to his hotel after that and we spent about a week together. He had to go back to Canada, but he told me he wanted me to stop working and after that he sent me money twice a month to pay for my rent, food, things for Alan, enough for me to live on without working as a prostitute.

I think I fell for him because he was tall, handsome, and about my age. Most of my other clients were old or fat or ugly or all of those things. Lee treated me well and I was really attracted to him. But after the first two weeks we began to fight about the "rock," and how much he was using. Now that I had feelings for him, I didn't like to see him go crazy with crack. And he didn't like it that I wanted him to stop. So we fought.

If I had known how much crack was going to take over his life, it would have been better if he never met me. But we went on together for years. He lived in Canada and worked as a building contractor. When things slowed down with his business, he would come down to Costa Rica, usually for two or three months. He would come down and he'd go crazy on crack and we'd party and argue. When he was back home in Canada, he would send me enough money to live on. He didn't want me to work and I didn't. I never cheated on him with any men, though I did fool around with girls once in a while. But it was nothing serious.

We got along pretty well most of the time, but we did have times when we fought, and I remember two different times when he went back to Canada with a black eye that I gave him! Mostly it was just my jealousy, but naturally there were the drugs and alcohol.

We went on that way for years and years, from around 2000 until 2006. He wanted to get married and for me to be able to go back to Canada with him, but we couldn't marry because I was still legally married to the Cuban guy. I had no way to find him to get a divorce. I couldn't get another visa to visit Canada because Canada had made it more difficult since my first trip. After putting in a lot of effort and spending a lot of money and time, Lee finally gave up. He finally found a Colombian woman to marry. She turned out to be very greedy and they fought even more than we did. About a year and a half after they married I saw him and he told me he had made a big mistake. Now, 20 years later, they are separated and live apart. I actually ran into him just recently, but whatever we shared together was gone except for friendship and memories.

CARMELA

It was very strange how my "relationship" with Carmela developed, because I had already known her for about three years. She was married and her husband was a good friend of mine. She wasn't a lesbian then, or if she was she kept it to herself. But although her husband was just a friend, she thought he was after me and that he wanted to be with me. So out of revenge or something she started to flirt with me. It felt strange because I wasn't attracted to her, but I did like her. But after a while I could see that she was starting to get serious about me, and we did end up having sex once, but just once.

She and her husband were both drug dealers, like a lot of my friends. She wasn't all that feminine even when she was married, but she gave that up entirely when she left her husband and basically just became a "butch." Most butches I know are very good to their girlfriends, and Carmela was very good to me and my son Alan even though I wasn't really her girlfriend. We didn't live together or have sex together other than that one time. But Alan and I both spent a lot of time at her house. She was very generous with him as well as with me. She bought him a PlayStation, a television, nice clothes, brand name Tennis shoes, and a lot of other things.

I was doing pretty well in that time. Carmela was very generous and I was also getting money from Lee, who came down for two months every year when the weather was worst in Canada but sent me money in between times. Carmela was giving me things, Lee was sending me money and so I didn't need to work. When Lee was in town I would spend a lot of time with him and he'd give me quite a bit of money. Sometimes I used to lie to her and tell her Lee was angry with me and didn't send me any money, and she'd give me money even though I actually was getting money from Lee too. I was very materialistic and greedy with her, I feel a little guilty about it now.

It all ended one afternoon when Alan and I were at her house visiting. Carmela was in the kitchen cooking and Alan was playing his PlayStation. I was in the back doing the laundry. All of a sudden we heard all this noise outside... sirens and the sound of cars. A van pulled up, full of cops, and cars with detectives and maybe a judge and some sort off officials. I can't say exactly, but they were men in suits. The cops burst into the house and one cop pulled out a pistol and pointed it at Alan, and told him "You! Outside!" And they put him in handcuffs, then they put Carmela in handcuffs and then me, just like Alan and Carmela.

We sat like that for hours while they tore apart the whole house and found a big bag of really good marijuana. We sat like that in handcuffs for three hours before they finally took us all in. Carmela told them that I only worked for her, that I was doing laundry, which I was at the time, lucky for me. They let Alan and me go but they kept Carmela. She got sent to jail and spent two and a half years in there. She's out now, and I we still stay in contact, but we're just friends.

CINDY

It was during my time with Lee that I met Cindy. Cindy was a bartender in the Avispa, a gay disco in San José. She was a very sweet person, very humble. I ended up moving in with her, but I didn't treat her very well, I used to hit her. I'm that way when I'm in love with someone, insecure, very jealous and I get violent. I was that way with Miguel and Nora too. Cindy used to give me all her money. She gave me her salary, her tips... everything.

Cindy was a butch, like all my girlfriends have been, but very nice looking, would have been a handsome man. There was this other butch, Mai, who was in love with her. Mayela had a very good job, some kind of manager with a big car dealer in San José. She was a lot older, fat, and not attractive. She was always buying presents for Cindy. Mayela knew nothing about me and Cindy. So Mayela bought Cindy a music system, and lots of other things. I told Cindy I wanted a microwave and Cindy told Mayela and Mayela bought Cindy a microwave and Cindy gave it to me. Then Mayela bought a microwave table. She bought Cindy a necklace and Cindy gave it to me. They never had sex or anything because Cindy didn't find her attractive and wasn't interested in her that way, but she kept getting presents. Mayela hoped that someday Cindy would be with her, but eventually Mayela realized it wasn't going to happen and stopped buying presents.

All the while I was getting the presents Mayela was buying for Cindy; I thought it was Cindy who was buying them. She told me she was borrowing money from people at the disco to buy these things. But one day when she left the room, she left her telephone out. I looked at the messages and I saw her thanking Mayela for all the gifts, for the microwave, the necklace, all that. When she came back in the room I attacked her and began choking her and shouting at her, "You have another lover! You didn't buy that stuff for me; some other woman bought it for you!"

"But I did it for you," she tried to explain "I never had sex with that woman, I don't care about her, I only love you," she told me. But I was crazy with jealousy and I threw her out of the house. After I calmed down, a day later, I let her back in. I still loved her and she loved me, and I understood that she did what she did for me.

The Avispa is a really nice place and Cindy was making pretty good tips, so at first we were doing pretty well. But Cindy was starting to miss work because we were partying too much. It didn't matter how much I did because I didn't have any real obligations other than taking care of Alan, and he wasn't much work. But all the drugs and late, late nights (and mornings) were too much for Cindy to do and hold down her job.

Eventually the Avispa fired her and I had to go back to working the El Jardin. Cindy didn't like that. She didn't like me going to San José and she didn't like me being with men. We lived near San Sebastian back then, and there was a corner nearby that was famous for selling crack. So Cindy said to me "Magdalena, I don't want you to go to San José, and I don't want you to go with any men. Please, buy me 50 grams (1 and ¾ ounces) of cocaine and I'll cook it and make crack out of it and sell it and give you the money." So I got her the cocaine and she made the crack and sold it. And she would always bring back exactly the right amount to me, at the start, at least.

But after several months I noticed that she wasn't eating and was getting thinner and thinner. Not only that, she was coming up short on the money she should have gotten from selling the crack. Sometimes she wouldn't come home at night, and this was happening more and more often. One of the other crack dealers told me she was smoking crack and I didn't believe it. I knew she snorted cocaine and so did I. I didn't believe she was smoking crack. But it wasn't long after that she was gone for several days and I saw her out on the streets with other addicts, and she looked just like them. I hated to do it because I felt responsible and I still loved her, but I had to kick her out. After that she just lived on the streets, begging and selling drugs if she had any extra.

It was about three years later that I heard that Cindy had cleaned up, wasn't doing any more crack or drinking, and that she was living with Fernanda! So I said, "Great!" And I thought: what a small world. My daughter stole Andrea from Fernanda, and Fernanda ended up with my ex-lover, Cindy! And it was really good for Cindy because Fernanda was very straight. She didn't drink or do drugs.

It was maybe two or three years later that I ran into Cindy by accident. She told me that she didn't love Fernanda and that she wanted to get back together with me. So she left Fernanda and moved in with me. But I could see that it was going to be bad for Cindy because I still liked to party. I still wanted to drink and do cocaine and I knew if she stayed around me she'd go back to drugs. So I told her she needed to get back with Fernanda, which she did. And I still see Andrea sometimes, and she's still good friends with Valeria. Andrea is a good person. Sometimes it seems like such a small world.

LAST YEARS AT HOTEL EL JARDIN

My last years at Hotel El Jardin weren't very good. There was a new owner and he was a drunk and a heavy cocaine user, always drinking rum, Flor de Caña. At least three times I saw him grab girls by the neck and throw them into the street. One time he tried to hit me too, and I told him that if he tried to touch me I would call the police and tell them about his drugs. He was a pig, and he had no reason to hit the girls. But still, it was my work and it was better than working out on the streets.

When he took over as boss it got a lot worse for all of us. He was always looking for a fight with the girls or with the customers, it didn't matter. It's hard for me to understand why somebody drinks and takes drugs just to be mean and angry, but that's what he did.

One time my friend Jenni came to me and told me he wanted a "show," that is, to have sex with the two of us. I didn't want to do it because I hated him, but I needed the money. So I went up to the room with them. But when I saw the size of his penis, I couldn't do it. I am very small, and it hurts me too much when a man is really big like that, so I told them no, I couldn't do it, and I left. From that day on he had it in for me, always insulting me, picking fights with me and yelling at me in front of all the gringos.

We used to do these lesbian shows with 10 or 15 girls at once. He'd close the door and collect the money from the customers. We were supposed to get all the money but we knew he was taking a lot of it. I was the star of the show because I had a lot of personality, and I could dance, and of course I actually liked having sex with some of the girls.

But the last night I worked there, he was very drunk and I was on my period, so I told him no, I wasn't going to dance. He got really mad and grabbed my drink and threw it across the bar. He told me that I had to dance. Then he grabbed my neck and tried to hit me. I told him if he hit me I'd call the police and tell them about his drugs. Well, he got me so angry I ended up calling the police and told them all about his drugs and everything. But I think he must have bribed them because they didn't do anything. I never went back after that. It was the end of me in Hotel El Jardin. I moved on to the New York Bar, or sometimes the Del Rey or the Key Largo. The El Jardin closed not too long after I left. I still see a lot of the girls from there. Most are still working. We are all getting older and it's not as easy as it was to find customers, but we still have to make a living somehow.

INTERVIEW WITH DENNIS

[I came to Costa Rica in 2002 on a family vacation with my wife and daughter. We did the typical tourist things... Manuel Antonio, the rainforest, Arenal, all those typical things. We were here for three weeks, and the last night we came back to San José to spend the night before we went to the airport the next day to go home. We were staying at the Hotel Doral on Fourth Ave. and Eighth St. My wife and daughter went to sleep and I was restless so I went for a walk. I had no idea that San José was anything more than a tourist spot, so I walked down the street about three blocks and saw that there was a bar open. The bar that was open was the El Jardin. I walked in the doors and that was my introduction to Hotel El Jardin, at about eleven-thirty on a Tuesday night.

As I walked in, I saw in basic first-grade printing "BJ Tuesday – BJ Thursday" I had no idea what it meant. I knew BJ meant blow job, but anyway, I went inside and saw Americans, mostly around 60, some younger, but mostly men who looked pretty desperate, pretty unsavory. Anyway, I fit in quite well (chuckles). I walked over to the bar, ordered a beer and started a conversation with a woman who called herself "China." I saw her many times later because after Hotel El Jardin closed she started going to the New York Bar.

Anyway, when I bought the beer, they gave me a little raffle ticket. Then they started doing drawings and I figured out that if they drew your number you won a free blowjob from any girl in the place, didn't matter if she was talking to somebody or what, you went upstairs and she would give you a blow job. The guy that owned the bar at that time was a guy named Bob Braddock. I later found out what a pathetic, drug addicted guy he was. I learned from the girls that he wouldn't let them work there unless they gave him free sex. And that was my first experience at Hotel El Jardin.

The one thing I remember about the guys that were there was their hygiene. A lot of them really stunk.

The one thing I saw there in the customers was people without roots or real connections... alcoholics, maybe drug addicted, people who had been thrown out by families, divorcees, people who were given money by their families to stay away... people that could never make any kind of relationship work, and kind of taking out that sadness, and it is kind of sad, on other gringos who they're drinking with, get ugly with when they've drunk too much, or the girls. And the girls are much easier. The gringos can just walk away from them, but the girls need the money. And just the lack of education, the lack of insight about who they are... I'm generalizing, generalizing, but what I see is at ten o'clock in the morning, these sad, rootless Americans, looking for something and hoping that they're going to find it in the drunk they're working on that day, possibly hooking up with some girl who more than likely will try to rob them. They're smart but they drink too much.

But going back to Hotel El Jardin, I still run into Magdalena downtown and there's another girl I still see from ten years ago. She's not really the same girl... she hasn't been a working girl for the last six or seven years. She's a grandmother... I trust her implicitly, but that doesn't mean she doesn't still ask me for things. Every time I see her she'll give me a list of things she wants me to bring back from the States. The last time that I saw her it was the biggest list that I'd seen so far. She wants me to go on Match.com, send in her picture, use my email but give them her phone number because she can't read or write English but she can speak it, so she wants them to call her and she can do the talking. She speaks very good English, she's been to the States...

typical Costa Rican education, learned her English at Hotel El Jardin, dealing with the gringos at Hotel El Jardin. We've had a relationship for about ten years, but I realize the relationship involves something... I can't come down here and give her nothing...expect to see her and give her nothing. Then it would just be... it simply would not work. She's barely surviving. She has her daughter and her daughter's children living with her along with her own thirteen year old still living in the house. Her son is out and married, but she said that marriage isn't working so she might end up taking in the son's children also.

So I see her when I come down, which is a few times a year. This time I brought her down a Texas Rangers tee shirt, which she asked for, and some perfume... Elizabeth Taylor "White Diamonds," which she asked for. And when I see her, I'll give her some money. She never asks for it. Sometimes it's forty dollars, sometimes only twenty, and she never asks for more. I think she gets a little money from the government, I'm not sure. We never went into detail about it.

She always had a very voluptuous body, but she's gotten bigger and bigger as the years have gone by. It's not about looks. But she knows what I enjoy. I know what she enjoys... it's the personal connection that makes it special for me, not just finding the hottest body to lay on top of. In my experience, the best sex is where you connect with her mentally

San José and Costa Rica have changed since my first visit. It's become more impersonal, more commercial. I think the Internet had quite a bit to do with it. When it was just word of mouth there weren't as many guys who even knew where Costa Rica was, let alone about the scene here, the prostitutes, the drugs and all that.

The guys that come down here haven't changed all that much. There are probably more young guys than before, but I wouldn't say they are any more cultured or educated. Where I come from in the States (Seattle area) I just don't run into men like I run into here. There's so much racism and misogyny, so much ignorance and negativity. I get depressed hanging around the barflies in Costa Rica. I can only handle San José for a few days then I have to get away. I have a good friend up near La Fortuna and I spend a week or two there between visits to San José. San José can be fun, but it can be depressing. I can only take it in small doses].

ALAN

My son Alan, who is in prison for murder, is my biggest sadness in life. I don't understand why he chose the path he chose, he seemed to have everything going for him. He was young, good looking, lots of friends, and plenty of girls. But growing up in Desamparados you meet a lot of bad people. When you look around and see that the only people who have anything in life are criminals, and these criminals are well respected, it's hard to convince a boy like Alan that he should study hard and finish school just to qualify for a job that pays a two dollars an hour and expects him to work sixty hours a week.

Alan was always very macho, even as a boy. He always wanted to be the boss. I hoped he would just live a quiet and honest life and stay out of trouble, but he didn't.

My son has brought me so much pain. Maybe it's my fault because of the kind of life I lived and where he grew up, with so many bad people around him. I tried to make enough to pay the rent and buy food and the things we needed, but even so, I was living the life of a prostitute. I would come home late pretty often, drunk and sometimes high. Maybe part of the problem is that I was using cocaine when I was pregnant. Maybe he got his violent streak from his father, Miguel. I just don't know.

My daughters didn't turn out violent like Alan and they aren't criminals. Maybe it's because Alan is a male. He was always hyperactive and as he grew up he was very macho, very aggressive, and always wants to be boss no matter where. And this is a problem because there are always others who want to be the boss, and there are always fights. He likes to think he's a real man but a real man wouldn't have two babies while he was in jail. It's not all his fault of course. His wife, Andrea, should have been taking the pill, but she is young and stupid. And now she has two babies, no money, and a husband in jail.

ALAN GOES TO PRISON

Alan was sixteen years old in 2006. One day I was in the house with him. I needed to go to my mother's house to wait for a phone call from Lee Sutton. He was still sending me money then. I didn't have a telephone where I was living at that time, and it was quite a ways to my mother's house, so I asked Alan to drive me there. Alan told me that he couldn't take me because he had to go somewhere to do a little business. I got angry with him but he left to do his business and I had to walk to my mother's.

Lee called me a little after lunch time, and we were talking when the 1 o'clock news came on television. The big story was that somebody had broken into the home of the Ambassador from Uruguay. They showed the car of the robbers and it looked like Alan's car. In fact, I knew it was his car because earlier that day he had two 1000 colon bills (worth 2 dollars) and after he gave me one he put the other in the windshield of his car. Sure enough, the car on television had a 1000 colon bill in the windshield. I knew it was my son Alan's car.

They still hadn't given the names in the news. I left my mother's and went back home. When I got there, the house was surrounded by my son's friends, waiting for me. They told me that yes, it was Alan in the news, and that during the robbery they had killed somebody. When they told me this I went berserk. I was so out of my mind I started banging my head on one of the lampposts. When I finally stopped they told me Alan had been shot and had two bullets in his arm. Then I heard on the radio that the robber was dead, that he had been shot in his back. This turned out to be wrong, but he did have two bullets in his arm.

I rushed to the hospital with Valeria and went to the room where my son was held. I was relieved to find out he was still alive, and not too seriously hurt. There were two police guards at the door and two more inside. I was able to look inside but they wouldn't let me enter. Outside the room were something like seven of Alan's girlfriends! Like I said before, he is very good looking and quite the ladies man. They were all crying. I asked them why they were crying and they said for Alan. All of them. I stayed about two hours but there was nothing I could do since they wouldn't let me go in.

That was the last time I would see him for four months. After I found out he was going to be alright my fear turned to anger. How could he be so stupid? Was this the way I was to be repaid for all that I had sacrificed for him? I could have gone to see him while he was in jail waiting for his trial, but I didn't because I was so angry with him.

I hoped they would set him free before the trial but they gave him 4 months preventative detention. Two people died in the robbery. One was an employee of the Ambassador and the other was an American who was watching from a balcony nearby. My son didn't kill anybody, he was just the driver.

I didn't go to the trial because I didn't feel like I could control myself and I might make some problem with the judge or something. So I stayed away. His trial was one day before my birthday and I prayed and prayed and I really believed that God would set him free for my birthday. It was just wishful thinking. After they sentenced him to fifteen years, I went to see him. I really thought they would set him free, but he got sentenced to fifteen years.

Alan and Andrea

When I thought he would get out, or get a short sentence, I didn't want to talk to him or see him. But when he got sentenced to fifteen years, I changed my mind. He was still my son no matter what, so I have been going to see him ever since he got sentenced.

He had barely been in the prison a week when he was beaten up by some of the other inmates and I felt like I needed to see him. His father, Miguel, had been to visit him before the trial, but only one time, and that was to try to sell Alan some shoes he (Miguel) had stolen. Great father he is. I haven't seen Miguel in a long time. Thank God for that.

So I started going every Sunday to visit him. He is my only son and I love him. I felt like he needed me, and he did. I would bring him some money to buy cigarettes and candy and toilet paper. The food is awful there, so I would bring him some good food from home every week.

I wasn't the only person visiting Alan in jail. There was a young girl, Andrea, who was a friend of one of his main girlfriends. She was fifteen at the time. Andrea's girlfriend's mother had forbidden HER daughter to visit Alan, and Andrea saw this as her chance, because she had always wanted Alan for herself.

Like I said before, Alan has a way with women. Most of his other girlfriends didn't bother. They were smart. But Andrea liked him enough to go visit him even though he was sentenced to fifteen years. But she wasn't eighteen yet and she couldn't visit him by herself. She had to go with her mother. I guess Andrea must have fallen in love with Alan, and maybe Alan fell in love with her too, I don't know. But no matter, the two of them decided they wanted to get married. Once they were married they could have conjugal visits twice a month and spend five hours together in private room. Great marriage.

Because they were both young, she had just turned sixteen and he was just seventeen, there was a problem. They needed permission from Andrea's mother, and her mother was against the idea. She said that my son was a delinquent. And that was true enough, I suppose. But Andrea was insistent and eventually her mother was persuaded to give permission. But she gave her permission only after I paid her $120 to get her to sign the papers. After she got the money, she was okay with her daughter marrying the "delinquent." My daughter, Valeria thought that was awful, that Andrea's mother would sell her daughter for $120, but that's what happened. So Alan and Andrea got married right there in the prison, with two friends of mine, Rafa and Vilma, acting as best man and maid of honor.

Now that they were married, they were allowed their conjugal visits. And it wasn't very long until Andrea became pregnant with my granddaughter Kiara. I already had several grandchildren by both Valeria and Gloriana. I was a pretty young grandmother the first time when Valeria had her daughter Graciela... only 30! Being a grandmother again was nothing new to me, but I felt it was a mistake for them to have a child. Andrea had no job and her "husband" would be in prison for several more years. What were they thinking? But what could I do? It wasn't like I could go in the room with them to make sure Alan used a condom!

THE NEW YORK BAR ERA

I was finished at Hotel El Jardin after my big fight with Bob Braddock. But I still needed to make money, so I went other places, usually the New York Bar. It was a pretty nice place, and nobody cared if we girls came in and sat around as long as we didn't bother the customers too much. Of course, plenty of the customers WANTED us to bother them. It was pretty much the usual mix of drinking, smoking, flirting, trying to make money and have a good time if we could. There were quite a few quite of my friends from Hotel El Jardin there and a lot of guys I had known for years.

I usually went there at night, but it was had a crowd during the daytime, too. It was mostly older gringos who drank a lot. Some of them wanted "company" in the afternoon so there were usually a few girls there too, hoping to make some money. I'm more of a night person and I didn't go there often in the afternoons.

It wasn't only gringos and prostitutes there. There were Tico men and gringa tourists sometimes. I speak some English and can flirt with the gringos, but there were plenty of folks there who spoke Spanish too, so it wasn't boring. All the bartenders were local so I could always talk to them or the other girls when I didn't have some possible customer to flirt with.

They had a security guy there in the bar, and it was a nicer part of town than the El Jardin. It was just down the street from the Del Rey, which is where the highest priced girls in town were working. When business was slow at the Rey you'd see some of the high priced girls wander in to the New York, and when there was nothing in the New York, sometimes I would take a walk around the Del Rey or the Key Largo, which was just across the street from the Del Rey. Mostly it was a waste of time, but once in a while some gringo would really like how I looked and I would make a pretty good amount of money. But most of the time it was just a waste of time going there.

The one thing I have going for me is I'm skinny. A lot of girls a lot younger than me are fat and a lot of gringos hate that, so I did alright once in a while even though I was pushing 40. But I felt more comfortable in the New York Bar than the Del Rey, so I spent most of my time there.

I left the El Jardin just a few months before it closed. It had been going downhill and a lot of the same girls and customers were moving away from there. There were quite a few spots you could work back in the early 2000s. There was the Piano Blanco the old Key Largo, Happy Days and the older version of the New York Bar. Back then you could even work the Presidente bar, if you didn't get too pushy. But the Piano Blanco was bulldozed and so were the old Key Largo and the first New York Bar. The owner of the old New York Bar took over when the Beatle Bar moved to Jacó, so we at least had that. The Key Largo turned into a night club, with live music and dancing. It was mostly the same girls as worked the Del Rey. They would go from one place to another, hoping to improve their luck.

I was still doing alright after I quit the El Jardin. There were still places to work and I still had some clients that would come down to Costa Rica and make a point of seeing me. It wasn't like when I was the star of the El Jardin, of course. When I was really young, back when I started, I never thought about getting old. I never thought about my future at all, really. I think the first thing that I noticed was when I was maybe twenty or so, and I wasn't the youngest girl in the bar anymore. There were some guys that liked the youngest girls they could get. It didn't really bother me because I was still very popular, but I did notice.

When I think about some of the things I did, it's obvious I wasn't thinking about the future. I should never have given up the house George bought me. But nobody can change the past. I usually don't worry much about the future, either. Things have gotten harder for me the older I get. Although I wasn't young like I used to be, business was still pretty good back from about 2000 to 2007 or so. But things haven't been very good for most girls I know since then. The New York Bar even closed a few years ago. I don't remember exactly when, but business just wasn't as good for anybody as it was.

There are not as many tourists now, and the gringos who live here are all getting older and sometimes they die. There was one old gringo who used to spend almost all day in the New York Bar, from when it opened at ten in the morning until he got so drunk some one of the other gringos would get him a taxi and send him home. Everybody called him Captain Benny because he wore this old sailor's hat all the time. It was really sad at the end. He didn't speak much Spanish and he was too old to care about women anyway. The gringos said that after a few hours in the bar, NOBODY could understand what he was saying. He would just sit there and talk to himself or towards anybody who walked by. He got to smelling pretty bad and I remember that once or twice he even pissed his pants sitting on the bar stool.

The owner never kicked him out, though. Maybe he was sorry for Captain Benny. Maybe he just didn't care. The owner drank a lot and when he got really drunk he would usually get angry. Nobody knew why. I remember one night I was there and the bar had a big crowd. The owner got mad about something and threw EVERYBODY out of the bar, yelling about something nobody understood. The bar was open again the next day and the bartenders said the owner was at home, sleeping it off.

I had some pretty steady customers there. One of them, a retired policeman named Paul, used to have me come over to his place every Saturday night and I would make enough to give Alan some money every week. This went on a pretty long time, but Paul must have gotten tired of me or found somebody else, because he stopped wanting to see me.

There were a few other clients of mine from the old days who are still around. Ted, one of the regulars, used to like to party with me, but his drinking and drugs have changed him and he gets crazy. I'm afraid to be with him now. I was really sad when the New York Bar closed, after all those years. Business was slow, but the owner kept it open as long as he could. He finally had to close it when he just couldn't pay the bills any more.

I always liked to go with regulars because you knew what you were getting. But my regulars weren't paying me enough to live on, so I was always looking for new customers. One night, a guy came in and offered to buy me a drink. I told him I'd have a beer, and we sat down to talk. While we were talking a guy came around selling roses. The guy bought me three roses and I thought it was very sweet. He acted very attentive and kind. He told me he was staying in a nice hotel down near Hospital Mexico [west of town, about five miles] and he wanted me to go there with him. I said okay, and we got in a taxi and drove there.

The hotel was an expensive one, very nice. We went up in the elevator to the fifth floor where his room was. Once I got inside the room I couldn't get over what a fancy place it was. I thought to myself how special it all was, and how nice it would be. But I was wrong.

I sat down on the bed and he went into the bathroom. I was waiting for him to come out, but five minutes passed, then ten, then fifteen, twenty... Finally, after almost half hour, I went into the bathroom to see what was taking him so long. I opened the door and I could smell marijuana and see a couple of lines of cocaine on a mirror he had laid on the sink. He told me to go take my clothes off and get on the bed.

I did what he told me, but I felt something was wrong, he was different. His eyes had a really strange look and the way he talked to me was different. He wasn't the same as he was back at the New York Bar. He saw me looking at the cocaine and he offered me some and asked if I'd like to smoke some of his mota with him, but I didn't feel like it because I had a bad feeling about him. I told him no thanks.

I went over and got undressed and lay down on the bed. He came over and started telling me what to do. He started by telling me he was going to put his dick in my mouth, which was okay. After a little bit of that he told me he wanted to fuck me in the ass. I told him no, I had never done that and I was afraid it would hurt. He told me I HAD to, and he grabbed me by the hair and tried to force me. He said "You're a whore, and that is what I'm paying for." I told him no, I didn't want to. He got angry and said I would either do as he said or he was going to kill me.

He grabbed me by the hair and dragged me over to the open window, and he said he would throw me out and kill me if I didn't do what he told me to do. He was drunk and drugged up enough to do it, and I was scared to death. He dragged me back to the bed by my hair. Although he was very drunk he was a lot bigger and stronger than I was. He dragged me onto the bed and put me on my stomach, and he was on top of me, with his legs on either side of me. Well, my legs were together and he couldn't do what he wanted while we were in this position, so he had to move off me to try to get me to spread my legs apart, but he was drunk and clumsy and I saw my chance while he was trying to get in the right position, and I kneed him right in the balls.

That caught him by surprise and howled and he jumped off of me. I was totally sober and he was drunk and drugged up, so while he was howling in pain I was able to get off the bed and run out the door before he could recover. I ran down the stairs, all five flights... I wasn't going to wait for the elevator. When I got downstairs, the guard asked me what I was doing there, naked. I told him what happened upstairs. He went and got me a jacket to cover myself, and went up to talk to the gringo. The guard came down with the gringo, who called me a liar and said I had tried to rob him and that is why he threw me out.

Of course none of that was true, but the guard didn't know who to believe. Even if he believed me, the gringo was a paying guest I was just a prostitute. The guard and the gringo went upstairs and the guard brought me down my clothes and my purse. My purse was empty except for my ID card, a couple of pictures and some personal things. I didn't have any money in there. I had no way to pay for a taxi and this was back before anybody had cell phones and I didn't know anybody who had a car to come get me. I ended up having to walk all the way from his hotel near Hospital Mexico to my house in Alajuelita, which was probably at least five miles, in the dark and in my high heeled shoes. What a horrible night that was.

MILENA

I haven't really had a boyfriend since Lee Sutton. My relationships have been with women, and really only one that lasted very long, Milena. We were together for a few years, and sometimes she still stays with me when she loses her job or needs a place for some reason. We aren't really lovers anymore, but she is still in love with me. I don't want to be in a relationship with her because it's bad for her.

We never had faith in each other. I don't understand why I never had faith in her. She's a good person, a very good person. She took very good care of me, more than my family. But I guess I was insecure about our relationship. I was always worried about her when she was away from me. I thought she would find somebody else, some other woman she liked more. I was very suspicious and jealous. If we'd go out, she couldn't say hello to anybody or I would get jealous and angry. I would get violent. In one year I think I beat her about ten times. I remember one time I cut her lip and then forced her to put guaro on it! I gave her black eyes, bruises and scars. And she STILL wants to get back together with me. I don't understand why. I treated her so badly.

I won't go back to how we were because I know how I am. I don't want to mistreat her but if we got back together I know I'd be just the same. One time I took some scissors and cut up all her clothes. I remember breaking up a piece of furniture she had that cost almost $1000 dollars one time. The last straw was when I took a knife and cut her. So finally she left, and stayed away for two months, afraid of me, and I don't blame her.

It's weird but when we were at home together I was very gentle and tender with her. I took care of all the housework and all the cleaning. I wouldn't let her lift a finger. And if somebody tried to mess with her I would defend her, go after whoever was bothering her. I wouldn't let anybody hit her. Only me.

Problems between Alan and Andrea

It's no surprise that my son Alan and his wife Andrea had their problems. What else could you expect from two teenagers without jobs or money and one of them in prison? So there were times when they would split up, though they were only together ten hours a month anyway.

It was during one of these splits that Margarita began to go with me to visit Alan. She was a pretty, young bartender at one of the bars I used to work, and we were friends. She was a little innocent when she started working as a bartender, but she saw what was going on around her and got propositioned pretty often. She saw other bartenders making more than a week's wages in an hour, and she didn't see any reason not to do the same. She just wasn't obvious about it, and neither are most of the bartenders who do a little work on the side.

And one night there was this gringo who wanted a threesome with the both of us, and since I like women and Margarita had already taken money for sex a few times and was my friend, she agreed to it and the three of us had sex together.

Not long after that I just happened to mention that I had a son, very handsome, who was in prison, and that I visited him on Sundays. I showed her a photo of him and she liked his looks. She told me she wanted to go with me next time to meet him. This was after she had sex with me! Pretty strange she had sex with his mother first. But I didn't care. She was pretty and good in bed, so I introduced her to my son. And it was a weird coincidence, but she knew one of the other guys who were in the robbery with Alan, and she had visited him before. It was very odd. He wasn't in the same jail though because he wasn't a minor like Alan. But she had visited him and they had sex in the prison. How weird! I guess she just likes men in prison or something.

This happened when Alan and Andrea were fighting, so Andrea wasn't visiting him. Alan wasn't doing without sex, though. Despite being in prison, there were ways to have sex without an official conjugal visit, just like I had with Fabi when I was in jail. A couple of the other prisoners would put up a blanket to make a little private area where Alan and whatever girl that came to visit him could have sex. Sometimes it was a sister of one of his friends in jail. He was in jail but he wasn't going without. It's really pretty common. A lot of women come to the prison for sex with the prisoners. It sounds crazy but that's how it is.

When Margarita met him, she really liked him and was willing to have sex with him like that, just behind a few blankets. I was embarrassed when they were together because I was right outside the blanket area and I could hear them grunting and groaning. It was hard not to laugh. I started to talk loudly to the other prisoners to hide the sound of the two of them from the guards and so I wouldn't have to listen to them myself.

More Alan and Andrea

Alan and Andrea didn't stay separated. On August 20th, 2011, his second child was born, another girl. I hope his children have a better life than their father. I hope there won't be obstacles and that they will grow up to be good persons. But I can't control their fates. I couldn't control Alan. What will be will be.

Every 15 days my son was allowed a conjugal visit from his wife, Andrea. They had special rooms for this. One time when Alan and Andrea were having sex, a guy and his wife were in the room next door. I was outside waiting for Andrea, and when she came out, she told me that Alan had gone to the room where the other guy was and had stabbed him 4 times with a homemade knife. I got really angry then because I didn't understand why he would do that. Andrea told me that the guy owed 3 joints to Alan. I got even angrier then. Why stab somebody for 3 stupid joints?

I was so angry that I wouldn't talk to Alan when he tried to call me. He was getting close to being eligible for parole, and I had suffered so much for him and he did that! I was devastated. Finally I cooled off a little a few days later and I spoke to him when he called.

"Mama, why won't you listen to me? Why won't you let me explain? You only heard what Andrea told you!"

So I said, "Okay, fine, tell me what happened."

So he said, "Mama, this guy and four other guys, five altogether, attacked me and beat me up and were going to rape me with a broom handle, they call the handle "Johnny." And one of them took out his dick and tried to force me to suck it. I was fighting back but there were five of them. Thank God three guards came and rescued me from the five. They took the five away and put them all in solitary as punishment. But they told me "This isn't over yet! The next time you see us we'll have knives!"

So Alan said "If I hadn't gone into his room first, he would have come for me." So I told him I understood that he had to protect himself before anything else, but he should try to avoid trouble because they will add more years to his sentence. He told me that it wasn't going to be a big problem because the guards were on his side and would stand up for him, say it was self defense.

So things had calmed down, and were almost back to normal when he called me again, in tears. Andrea had left with the girls and didn't tell anybody where she was going. She had left him. She has family in Golfito and he thought that's where she went.

She didn't have any job or any money and had two babies, a 2 year old and the other just two months. I wouldn't be surprised if she was with the man she was seeing when she and Alan were separated for a few months. I really think the baby might be his, not Alan's, and Alan feels the same way. We don't know for sure that she left with the ex boyfriend or that the baby is his, but just by chance I was on the bus one day and I saw them talking together, so I think she might have gone with him. Alan is very sad because she took his two daughters. The youngest baby may not be his, but Kiara is and he's very sad about it. I know it's been rough for Andrea, but she didn't have to have a baby while her husband was in jail, let alone two. How stupid can you get?

Now Alan has been in prison more than 7 years and we were hoping they would release him after six years since it was his first problem with the law and they usually they cut the sentence in half, but they haven't let him out yet. Every time there is a hearing, I get my hopes up, and every time they haven't set him free. I don't know what's going on. Other men get released after half their sentence, but not Alan. Maybe it's because of whose house they were robbing, a rich, important man. I just don't know.

Right now I'm hoping they will release Alan soon. He is coming up on 8 years this summer. I have been going almost every week to visit him, on Saturday or Sunday. One week Saturday is visiting day and the next week it's Sunday. I try to take him some food, because the food is so bad there, and some money to buy toilet paper, toothpaste and other things. I have a gringo who has been helping me with money for my son, but he just told me he can't help me any more. I don't know where I'll get the money but I guess I will have to try working more. I can usually find some customer but all I can depend on are a few cheap gringos that I really don't like. But I am older now and I can't be very particular.

THE JACÓ INCIDENT

Back when Margarita was still going to visit my son in jail, as his girlfriend more or less, we were talking one night about how bad business was in San José. She said she had Thursday and Friday off from work, so we decided to go try our luck in Jacó. We had a little money, so when we got to Jacó we rented ourselves a room. We took it easy for a while and when it got to be early evening we got dressed up and went to the Beatle Bar to look for "clients." We ran into some friends of mine that I hadn't seen in a long time. One of them was Vera, a girl I knew from Hotel El Jardin. Back then the Beatle Bar sold these cheap drinks for women, just vodka and some kind of juice. So we were talking, joking, getting high and just having a good time, and before we knew it the bar was closing and we had to leave.

Margarita and I left the bar with Vera. We were walking through a little park near there and there was this young, nice looking gringo who asked us where we were going and asked us if we wanted to party. We said sure, what did he have in mind? He said he had a bottle of tequila and some coke, and we said that sounded good. He said "But where?" And Vera said "We can go to my apartment." Vera lived in Jacó, so off we went to her apartment with the gringo.

Once we were there it wasn't long before we were all naked and fooling around, drinking and doing coke. I remember Vera had this little dog and for some reason it didn't like me and kept barking at me, only at me, not at Margarita or the gringo.

After a while I remember Margarita and I were in the bedroom with the gringo, and I remember Margarita was giving him head and I was licking Margarita. Vera had never been with a woman before so she joined in and we were all having a good time. After a while though, it was just the gringo and I alone together. Margarita and Vera were in the other room. I think the gringo liked me because I was very hot and horny. So we spent quite a while alone in the bedroom.

Finally I was getting tired and I told him I needed to take a break. I went in to take a shower and he went into the living room where Vera and Margarita were. While I was in the shower I heard the gringo start shouting, very angry. "Where's my money!!!??? Give me back my money!!!" he was shouting. I had been in the room with him all the time. I got out of the shower and I told him I didn't take his money. He had paid me $60 and we were in the room having sex all the time. So I asked Vera what was going on and she said in Spanish, "Take it easy, I got $1500 dollars, I'll take care of it." The gringo didn't speak Spanish so he didn't understand what she said. I told the gringo I didn't have his money, only what he paid me. Vera told Margarita and me to just go, get out, go back to our hotel room. Vera said she would deal with the gringo. He was very angry and said he was going to call the police. Vera said "Fine, go ahead! The only thing the police will do is throw you out of the apartment!" And the gringo was still pissed off but he didn't call the police because he knew he couldn't prove anything and even worse he had a lot of drugs on him, bags of cocaine, so he finally left.

Margarita and I went back to Vera's apartment the next day and she gave us our share of the money. I felt bad for the gringo. He didn't deserve to be robbed, but I wasn't going to turn on Vera. And even if I wanted to I couldn't prove she took the money any more than the gringo could. But after all Vera put us through I took my share of the money, $400 and Margarita got $400 too. I didn't like it, but Vera put us all in danger with the gringo. He could have had a pistol for all we knew. I'm not a thief but I needed the money and with what Vera put us through, Margarita and I deserved it as much as Vera did.

That was a few years ago, and since then Alan got another girlfriend who was visiting him every week for a while, and I didn't always have to go. I would give her the money and she would go. To visit takes up most of the day. I have to take the bus into San José, walk half an hour to the bus that goes to the prison, then the bus to the prison takes another hour. Then I have to wait in line, which can take an hour, visit, then another hour back to San José and then another hour back home. A very long day and I was glad to have somebody go see him instead of me. But Alan got a surprise visit from Margarita a few weeks ago, and the new girlfriend showed up, and she broke up with him. Always drama. But she forgave him and she's back visiting him again. Thank God I don't have to go every week now.

My Daughter, Gloriana

Gloriana's father visited her this week. It's been years since his last visit, and he's probably seen her maybe five times since she was grown up. He's never been a father to her, but for some reason he decided to visit her.

Gloriana and I get along pretty well. She has a sweet disposition, not like Valeria. But just like Valeria she got pregnant at fourteen. I wasn't quite as upset as I was with

Valeria. Maybe it's because she wasn't the first to make me a grandmother.

She had a daughter she named Rachel. The father was some Nicaraguan guy in the neighborhood, the son of a friend of mine. Of course he had no job and didn't take any responsibility for Rachel. There's a joke here: Sex is magic. A baby appears and the father disappears.

Gloriana was pretty irresponsible in getting pregnant, but she has been a decent mother. She must feel I was somehow responsible too, because she lived with me for the next three or four years and I paid the bills. This was from 2001 to about 2003 or 2004. I was getting money from Lee Sutton and working a little at Hotel El Jardin, so I could afford it.

When Rachel was born, she had a problem with one of her feet. It was crooked. The treatment the baby needed was very rough, and Rachel would cry horribly. Neither I nor Gloriana could stand to hear it, so my friend, Marilyn was the one that took the baby to the hospital for treatment. Thank God the treatment succeeded and Rachel's foot is fine now.

About a year and a half after Rachel was born, Gloriana got pregnant again. This time she didn't even know who the father was. Gloriana was happy to be having another baby, but I wasn't happy about it. She gave birth to a son she named "Alan" after her brother. I didn't think it was fair for her to keep having babies and for me to have to support them.

Thank God Gloriana found a boyfriend soon after that, and he actually had a job! She moved in with him and soon she was pregnant again. His name was Marco and he was very much in love with Gloriana. They lived together for three years and eventually got married in 2009. But their marriage didn't last. They were married only about a year when they separated and eventually divorced. Marco was a good husband and father, but Gloriana said he wasn't "exciting" enough for her.

Now she's with another guy Marco. The New Marco works construction. He's not nearly as nice a man as the first Marco. He beats her and the kids. I guess he's exciting enough for her. She has split up from him a few times but they always ends up getting back together. The first Marco, her ex, heard about him hitting the kids and he took custody of their daughter Mariana. Rachel has come to stay with me a few times when things were bad. But if Gloriana wants excitement, she has it with Marco number 2. She has had two children by him, one boy and one girl. The girl was born just recently, making a total of five. She jokes that she wants to have eleven, enough for a football team. I think she's crazy. Rachel is a good kid, and the baby is just a baby, but her other kids are monsters, little brats. Gloriana is easy going and it doesn't seem to bother her. They would drive me crazy.

Although I get along with Gloriana better than I do with Valeria, neither one of them bothered to remember me on my birthday or Mother's Day. Not even a phone call. This really hurts me. My own mother was a terrible mother to me, especially when I was very young. But I still visit her and I never forget her birthday or Mother's Day.

A few weeks after last Mother's Day I was walking to the grocery store when I saw Gloriana walking towards me with her new baby in her arms. There was nobody else in the street. I didn't feel like talking to her but I still love her, even though she doesn't seem to care about me. As we got closer, she called out to me, "Ma!" So since she spoke first, I answered her, "Come here... let me see your new little monster." I could see that she didn't like the way I said that, but she came over anyway.

Well, this was the first time I saw my newest grandchild. It would have been normal for me to kiss him, and to kiss my daughter on the cheek, but I didn't because I was still angry about how she didn't even call me on my birthday or Mother's Day. But we talked a while and she told me how angry she was with Rachel, who was twelve. Rachel had just failed the fifth grade. She had passed all her subjects except one, which was her behavior. She had been very disrespectful towards her teacher, and she had to repeat the fifth grade. Gloriana was angry about it, not the least because it costs a fair amount of money every year to buy uniforms, books, and everything. When we finished talking and she went one way and I went another.

A few days later at about two in the afternoon Gloriana's daughter, Rachel, and her son, Alan, showed up at my door, soaking wet from the rain and crying. They all needed a place to stay, Gloriana and the baby included, because Marco Two was going crazy again, getting violent. Well, I felt bad for the children, but I told them no, I didn't have room for them, which was true enough, but I was also tired of how Gloriana ignores me until she needs something. And anyway, I was sure it would be just like it always had been before: Gloriana would come running to me for a day or two then kiss and make up with Marco Two and nothing would change. I was fed up with the whole thing. So in the end they ended up staying with Valeria for that night. And sure enough, she went back to Marco Two a day later. Valeria and Gloriana deserve each other. Neither one cares about me unless they need something. I wasn't worth calling on my birthday or on Mother's Day.

ESTHER

I have known Esther for years, going back to the New York Bar days. I always got along with her, we used to joke and she was always friendly, kissing my cheek, patting my butt... I knew she wanted to have sex with me, at least do a threesome with me and a customer. I always avoided it mainly because she's pretty old. So am I, I know, but she's not that good looking. But at the same time I thought maybe she'd be good, maybe it would be good sex, so I wasn't really against the idea.

I was in El Capitan Bar one night, drinking and hoping for a customer. There was this gringo sitting at the bar, and I said hi to him and he said "hi" back. He was sitting beside Jenni and so I sat on the other side. Jenni asked him if he wanted "company" and he said no, finished his beer and left. No big deal, part of the job. I went over to say hi to my friend Maria and she was with a client of hers, who bought me a beer. I was almost finished with it when Esther came in. I went over to say hello and then went back to finish my beer with Maria and her friend. While I was finishing my beer, the gringo from before came back in and was sitting at the corner of the bar next to Esther, and they were talking together. On my way to the bathroom I stopped and said to her "What are you doing with my husband?" Just joking around, you know. And the gringo said "Yeah right! I'm not anybody's husband." Then I said to him "Then what are you doing with my wife?"

And all of a sudden he got interested. "How's that? She's your wife?"

I said "No, we aren't married but we've always wanted to be together, but never had the chance."

He said "Really, you two want to have sex together?" So I told him about how we had known each other for years and had always talked about our fantasies but we had never done it because we had never had a customer who took us both to bed at the same time. I was trying to drum up some business for me, for us, so I padded the story a little. He smiled and said, "Well, I think I can help you with your fantasy!" And I looked over at Esther and her eyes went wide open!

After a while he said to me, "Give her a kiss!"

"No... We'll do sex but no kissing!" But he seemed to really want to see it. Well, I was a little drunk and I needed the money, so I thought "what the hell" and so Esther and I kissed. We probably spent about two more hours drinking and joking around when the gringo said "Let's go to my room." We said okay, should we call a taxi? And he said he was staying at the hotel right across the street. So we crossed the street and went up to his room.

It's my habit, my routine to shower before and after sex, I'm very particular about that, but Esther didn't shower either before or after, and I didn't want to go down on her because I knew she wasn't going to smell good. So I gave head to the gringo and had Esther lick me. And actually she was really good at it! It was really good! I actually came three times with her licking me, then I got on top of her and came two more times while we were rubbing against each other. The gringo was really happy with us. It was his first time with two women, and the sex was real, not fake like most of the lesbian shows they have in night clubs. I came six times... it can't get much more real than that!

MY MOTHER

After all these years my mother is still with Juan. She's still an alcoholic, though he doesn't drink anymore. He used to be a horrible alcoholic, pass out in the streets, even sleep in the streets, but he doesn't drink now. And it's strange, but sometimes when one of my daughters or I need some money, my mother will say no but Juan will help us. He's actually very kindhearted, but he has a very dirty mind. He doesn't have any respect for us, always trying to touch our tits or pussies. My daughter, Gloriana had to move in with them for a while when she split up with her Marco #2, and she was always worried about Juan. She has a teenage daughter, Rachel, and Juan would always try to touch her where he shouldn't. That's one of the reasons my mother won't let me live in the same house with her and Juan. She's jealous and thinks Juan will try something with me, and she's probably right. When I think about it I want to cry, because my mother will never change. She'll never admit that she's been living with a rapist, a child molester. He's very nice in some ways but he's a child molester. And she has no shame about living with him. He has a very dirty mind. He's old but he's still horny, and when he wants sex he'll buy my mother a bottle of guaro and get her drunk. And I can hear them sometimes and I can tell he's hurting her, but that's their life, it's her choice to live that way. She cares more for him than for her own children. She has given birth to sixteen children, two stillborn and three that she gave away. What a mother I have.

Interview with Mama

"My childhood was very bad. We lived in Heredia. We went without food. My father didn't work. He cheated on my mother. When he came home he beat my mother and the children. He beat me. I remember the police came and took him away one time. I left school in the third grade. It was because there wasn't any food. I went to work picking coffee. It was because I was the only one old enough. I was the oldest. So I had to stop my studies in order to earn some money to feed my mother and all my brothers and sisters. They were all younger and it was up to me.

"I left home when I was fourteen years old, when I got married to a man twenty-three years old. I was with him for five years. When we got married, none of my family went to the wedding, only his family. After we were married we went to live with his parents. I can't remember how old his parents were, but they died very soon after we moved in with them. I stayed with my husband because he was my husband and we were married in the church.

"When I was fifteen, I had my first child, Patricia. After Pati, I had Rodrigo, who was named after his father. Then I had Magdalena. After Magdalena came Yorleny. [At this point, a discussion started back and forth between Magdalena and Mama about who came next and it seemed nobody was exactly sure. They finally decided the after Pati came Rodrigo, then Magdalena, then Yorleny. The last child by Rodrigo Sr. was Isabel.] After I separated from Rodrigo Sr. I lived in Moravia. In Moravia I found work in a restaurant. I served food and cleaned up. I didn't have any boyfriend at the time. After Moravia I moved to a hotel in San José. Pati and Isabel stayed with their other grandparents.

"I got together with Juan then. We are still together. With Juan I had "Chico," Juan junior, and Danilo. We also had three children who were stillborn. Thanks to God that all the rest are well and healthy now, they are all very good."

[But Rodrigo is in prison, right?]

"Yes! Always in jail! That one is terrible; he's famous for being bad. He was always a problem child. He's has been in jail for years. He walks with a limp because somebody shot him in the leg three times. He has ten more years to go on his sentence. I don't go visit him. I didn't teach him to rob. I didn't teach him to steal cars. When he called me I told him "Don't call me Mama!" I didn't teach him to mug people. I didn't teach him to rob houses. I didn't teach him to steal cars. I'm ashamed of him!"

[And what about Alan?]

"Poor boy! His mother adored him! But he's terrible as well. I think when he gets out he'll probably just go back in. I don't visit Rodrigo because he's forty-eight, he's an adult now, and he's not going to change. And it's the same with Magdalena and Alan. She cares very much for him but he doesn't care about her. If he cared about her he wouldn't do the things he did. She always treated him well, did anything for him.

The funny thing about Rodrigo is that his father was actually a policeman!"

[You mean... his father wasn't Rodrigo Sr.?]

"No! The father was actually a policeman, a big man, about your size." [I am a little over six feet tall.]

[I asked her what she thought about Magdalena working as a prostitute.]

"Well, it's not an easy life for her and she does what she has to do to live. I never did that... never in my life. I worked as a waitress *or as a cook. I cleaned houses, but never worked as a prostitute. I used to love to go out, I loved to dance. I would sneak out of the house when I was younger and my father would beat me when I came home. I always loved to dance and I loved to go out and dance all my life but I never went with just any man. But Magdalena is a good person, with a very big heart."*

KEY LARGO INCIDENT

One night back when the New York Bar was still open, there was nobody in there and I decided to try the Key Largo. I don't usually like to go there because the girls there are younger but I didn't have any money and I wasn't going to make any in an empty bar, so I thought I would go try my luck at the Key Largo. I went and sat down on a stool and watched the people dancing. A gringo came over to say hi to me, said "Hola flaquita" *[hello slim]* and I smiled at him and said "Hola gordito" *[hello chubby]* because he was a little heavy. So he asked me my name and I told him and he asked me if I wanted to go with him. And I said, of course, that's why I'm here! He asked me how much I charged, and I looked at him and thought he didn't look like he was going to pay a lot, so I decided not to ask for too much, and told him $50. He told me he'd pay me $70. And I said to myself, uh oh, something weird here. I said, well, what are you going to do to me, or what do you want me to do? And he said it was a secret in his room. So I told him I was afraid that he wanted to do something weird with me, or to me. He said no, don't worry, I'm not going to do anything to you, I just have fantasies that I want. So I said "You aren't going to hurt me?" and he said no, I want YOU to hurt ME. Well, that's not my preference but I said okay, if that's what you want.

So we went back to the Del Rey where he was staying and went up to his room. When we got in the room he said he was going to go to the bathroom. I said "okay." Then he said not to take off any of my clothes. Well, okay, I said, I won't take anything off. So he went into the bathroom, and he was in there for a while, longer than I thought it would take for him to just take a pee. When he came out, he was had on women's underwear... a bra and panties, the whole bit. So he asked me "Do I look sexy?" Well, what could I say? I said yes, he looked very sexy. I thought maybe he was going to give the lingerie to me as a gift but no, that wasn't it.

He got out a paddle made of wood, very hard and gave it to me. Then he lay face down on the bed and told me he wanted me to call him dirty names and whack him on the ass with the paddle. I said "Seriously?" and he said yes. Hard? Yes, hard. I said I couldn't, I didn't want to. He told me that was what he wanted, and that was what he was paying me for. So I thought to myself, $70 is decent money and I began hitting his butt with the paddle, hard. He began to shout "Yes, Yes! More, more!" And his butt cheeks were getting really red, but his dick was getting really hard, he was getting really turned on. So he turned over and told me that now he wanted me to suck him off, and I said okay and began sucking him but he said he didn't want to come in my mouth, he had a different position he wanted to finish with. So when he was getting close to coming he said to stop, and to take off my clothes. I always shower beforehand and when I came out he said to go back in the bathroom. I said why? I already showered. He said not to worry, but to wait for him in the bathroom.

He came into the bathroom, and the shower was nice and big, and he lay down on the floor of the shower and I asked him what he wanted to do? He said he wanted me to piss on his face! So I said "Seriously? I can't do it, I just can't do it!" And he said "I'll give you a propina (tip)." This wasn't something I wanted to do, but money is money and I needed money, and if that was what he wanted and he was going to pay for it, I would try to piss on his face. It wasn't easy, it felt so strange, but after a while I was able to let go and I did a nice big piss right on his face while he masturbated, and that's how he came.

He asked me to turn on the shower and he cleaned up and thanked me and told me he was very happy and gave me a nice tip. He told me he was leaving for the United States the next day but that he wanted to see me again the next trip to Costa Rica. Next time, he said, he wanted me to shit on his face! Oh my God! I prayed to God that he would never come back to Costa Rica and I haven't seen him since. My prayers were answered!

POST JARDIN

A bunch of things changed for me around 2005. Hotel El Jardin closed a little while after I quit in 2004. I was still getting money from Lee Sutton but the money I was earning at the New York Bar wasn't as good as what I had made at Hotel El Jardin. Right about the time Alan got arrested and went to prison, Lee finally got frustrated trying to get me a visa to come to Canada. The money from Lee stopped and I was now trying to spare some money for Alan in prison so he could buy toilet paper, some candy, whatever.

I had always been pretty self-sufficient till then, but there were times when business was slow or I was sick and things got rough. There were times when I didn't have the money for the rent, so I would need to move in with somebody for a while. One of those times, I moved in with Gloriana, Marco Two and the kids. It was alright for a while. In order to help pay expenses, I kept working. And it's just part of the work that sometimes people buy me drinks. It's all part of the scene and I like to have fun. So sometimes I would come back to the apartment and I had been drinking. Marco Two didn't like this and he asked me to leave. It was okay with me because I was working nights and the children would play and make noise when I was trying to sleep. Her kids are pretty much little monsters, anyway, spoiled brats.

After living with Gloriana I went to live with Valeria and Liliana. They had been together for six years, off and on. They were always fighting, breaking up, and then getting back together. Valeria worked as a manager in a little restaurant and Liliana worked in a butcher shop. The two of them were separated when I moved in, so it was just Valeria and Graciela, who was fourteen at the time.

I stayed with them only for a few weeks. Liliana moved back in and I don't get along with Liliana, so I moved out about a week later. They only gave me a little corner of the kitchen to sleep in, and I was paying half the rent.

INTERVIEW WITH VALERIA

[I remember when we when we lived in the house that George bought for her. We spent a lot of time with him, my mother, my sister and I, when he was in Costa Rica. My sister Gloriana was still a baby. The house was nice and everything was calm when George was around. Then my mother met Miguel, my brother

Alan's father, and things got worse. Miguel and my mother drank and fought all the time.

Drinking and doing drugs, all that. They left Gloriana and me alone with babysitters, friends, different ones, whoever was available. Sometimes we wouldn't see Miguel and my mother for days. They would be out drinking and doing drugs. I remember one time they left us in the house with some woman who stole almost everything in the house, things from the kitchen, lamps, all sorts of things.

They were always fighting. When she was pregnant with Alan, he beat her. He held a gun to her head one time, cut her with a kitchen knife, pulled her hair. I was afraid, naturally. But all of the violence was between them. Miguel never hit us children. But it hurt me to watch that, and it scared me. I hated that she let it happen.

Mostly they didn't pay us much attention. The only time my mother was affectionate with us was when she would come home drunk. Otherwise she either paid no attention to us or would be hard with us. The older I got the more I resented it. I resented it a lot. My sister is more sentimental than I am. I'm not talking to my mother any more, but my sister is. I'm harder than Gloriana. Maybe it's because I'm the oldest. Anyway, I never felt like she cared about me, I felt neglected. When they would fight Gloriana and I would shut ourselves up in a bedroom to stay out of the way.

Even now she's a lot the same. She still drinks and I don't want my daughters to see her that way. Graciela's father lives in Cartago. When I got pregnant with Graciela I was 14. The father was a boyfriend, but after he found out I was pregnant it was the end of our relationship. He didn't want the responsibility and he didn't have much to offer. He wasn't much older than I was and he didn't have a job or any way to support me and my baby. I was too young myself, but I didn't have any choice. Abortions are illegal and birth control is expensive, and it was too late for the pill anyway. We didn't have much of a real relationship anyhow, we just had sex one night when I was a little drunk and I got pregnant. When I told my mother, she got really angry with me. She beat me when I told her.

I stayed with my mother and her lover, Francisco, who was a taxi driver. That lasted for about three months. Then I left with an older man, about thirty, who took care of me while I was pregnant and almost a year after that. When I was seventeen I had my first experience with a woman, Laura. We were together six years. I grew up around lots of lesbians, my mother for one. To me it was nothing unusual. Laura and I fought a lot. We both drank too much and we would fight a lot. At first she earned most of the money. I couldn't work much even if somebody wanted me to because I had a baby to take care of. But after Graciela got a little older, especially when she started school, I was able to find some work. I don't mind working and I always try to do a good job. The job I have now is because my first boss gave me a good recommendation. I don't have enough "colegio' [high school] to get this job but my old boss recommended me and I got hired, and now I'm manager here.

And I manage a restaurant and I am working with my boyfriend and even my father [Eduardo]. I was able to hire him and now he has a steady job too.

After Laura and I broke up I started going with Liliana. At first we got along well enough. We spent eight years together. I didn't drink any more but Liliana and I would fight too. She was very jealous and possessive. But we were still together for eight years.

[Q: what do you think of what your mother does for a living?]

Prostitute? It's nothing special. It's nothing to be proud of, but most people I know don't think it's a horrible thing to do. I never considered it, though. I never wanted to sleep with men for money. It isn't the sex that bothers me, it's the kind of life the women live. There is a lot of alcohol and drugs and it's just not the kind of life I want to live. I have a stable, secure job. I'm not rich but I don't worry about where the rent will come from every month.]

VALERIA AND LILIANA

Valeria was always a strong willed child. She was stubborn and selfish. When she was a little girl, she wasn't that much of a problem, but as she grew older I had more and more problems with her. She was disrespectful to me and rebellious. She knew how I had gotten pregnant too young and ended up a prostitute, but she went ahead and got pregnant at fourteen anyway. We had a big fight and she ended up moving out of my home. We haven't been on good terms since then. We were never best friends, but we did speak to each other at least. And she would still ask me to baby sit Graciela once in a while. She would include me in her life when I could do something for her.

She had an older boyfriend that she moved in with a few months after she got pregnant. They were together about a year after Graciela was born. After she split up with him, she decided she was a lesbian and had a girlfriend called Laura. They were together for years. After Laura, there came Liliana. They were together for years, too.

Valeria Cheats and Gets Knocked Up

Valeria is in her thirties now. We don't get along but she's like me in some ways. She moves a lot and there's always drama in her life. She was with Liliana for several years before she turned up pregnant. A woman in a lesbian relationship isn't supposed to get pregnant, but Valeria did. It turns out that she was having an affair with an eighteen year old who worked with her at the restaurant, named Joaquin. He was just eighteen when he became a father, but Valeria's affair with him started when he was only fifteen. He's only three years older than her daughter, Graciela! So while she was living with Liliana she was carrying on with this boy all the while in secret. Valeria and Liliana had split up and gotten back together several times before Valeria got pregnant. They had a big fight when Liliana found out Valeria was pregnant and Liliana left. Once Liliana left, Joaquin, the baby's father, moved in.

That only lasted a short time until Liliana showed up unexpectedly and Joaquin, the boyfriend, was there with Valeria. She had a knife and she wanted to stab Valeria and kill the baby and Joaquin. Valeria was three months pregnant and they said she had a cyst in her ovary and her pregnancy was high-risk, so she called my sister Patricia to help her and Graciela move. All of this during the rainy season, too. Because of Valeria's high-risk pregnancy, Pati had to carry almost everything herself. Pati is a very kind hearted person, too kind hearted, really. Valeria's new place was close to where my mother lived but Liliana didn't know where she was living.

At the time I told everybody to wait a week or so and Valeria and Liliana would be back together, and I was right. They were soon back together and Joaquin was back living with his parents again. Liliana was jealous of Joaquin, of course, but when they got back together she thought she was going to get a chance to play the part of the baby's father. But Joaquin wasn't the only problem. Valeria began to be jealous of Graciela. She thought that Liliana was a little too interested in Graciela. It wasn't Graciela's fault. She was always a pretty little girl, but as she got older, she wasn't a little girl any more, and Valeria was jealous. She probably had reason to be. Liliana would buy Graciela presents and paid more attention to her than Valeria thought was right.

It all ended up in a big mess. Graciela wasn't only getting attention from Liliana, but there was a neighborhood boy about a year older than she was, José, who happened to be the son of one of the local drug dealers. Although he was young, he definitely wasn't innocent. He was still in his early teens but had already killed somebody. He was with two friends when they assaulted another boy, stabbing him. He was the one who stuck the last knife in him, and killed him. And he didn't even spend any time in jail. And my son Alan, who was also in his early teens, was sentenced to fifteen years for just driving the car for the robbers who ended up killing somebody during a burglary. Alan and the robbers had the bad luck to try to rob an ambassador. So for being the driver, he got fifteen years. And José, who actually did the killing didn't even go to jail. José was lucky that his victim was just another "delinquent." The police and courts didn't much care.

When José started to hang out with Graciela, Liliana didn't like it at all. She was jealous of José. Valeria was already jealous because Liliana was paying too much attention to Graciela. When Graciela started seeing José, it gave Valeria an excuse to throw Graciela out of the house. I think it was mostly jealousy, not because she cared much about what Graciela was doing. After her mother threw her out, Graciela moved in with me. I lived very close by so it wasn't any big deal, but I don't think it was right. Liliana brought nothing but trouble to my family. My brother Danilo wanted to beat her up because she beat. So did my mother, but I'm glad she didn't try, she isn't young any more.

GRACIELA

Graciela moved in with me when Valeria threw her out. Valeria and Liliana split up forever a little while after that, but Graciela was enjoying her freedom and still seeing José. She had dropped out of school by then. She was just past fifteen. I didn't like what she was doing, but even if I wanted to, I couldn't watch her twenty four hours a day. I had to work and make money for us to eat and pay the rent. I kept working like I always did.

Not long after she moved in with me, I went out with some of the other girls and one thing led to another and I ended up away from the apartment all that night and the next day. I called to check on Graciela and she said she was with my mother. I thought she was safe, and I didn't worry about getting back home in a hurry. It was about two the next morning when I came back to the apartment. I'd been awake a long time, had a lot to drink and all, and I was very tired. I went into the bedroom and I saw Graciela lying on the bed. She was taking up most of the bed, so I nudged her to move over. She didn't move. I pushed her harder and called her name, "Graciela! Graciela!" but she didn't move. I turned her face to me and lifted up her eyelids and all I saw were the whites of her eyes. That's when I noticed she had vomit all over her face.

I called my sister Pati and we called an ambulance. It came and they took Graciela to the hospital. I went with Pati and Milena up to Valeria's place to tell her that her daughter was in the hospital. I was angry with her, and told her it was all her fault for throwing Graciela out on the street with nothing, and that Graciela had been drinking and doing drugs... cocaine, marijuana and sniffing glue. I told her this was HER daughter and HER fault for throwing her out of the house. She didn't say a thing. She may have thought it was my fault Graciela was hanging out with the wrong people, but with Pati and Milena there, she wasn't going to take on the three of us.

When Graciela was recovered enough, she moved back in with Valeria for a few days, but before a week was out she was back living with me. I asked her who gave her all the alcohol and such that made her so sick. I was thinking it was José or Oscar, but it was my own mother along with Juan! They were giving her rum. What a fucking family I have.

LOBSTER NIGHTMARE

When Graciela was living with me, I had a client named Gary whom I met through my friend Teddy. Gary wanted me for a girlfriend but I wasn't interested. He wanted me to spend all my time with him and that wasn't what I wanted. I'm too independent for that. But I needed the money, so I would go see him a few times a week. He always wanted me to stay longer and I always wanted to leave earlier, so neither of was totally happy, but that's how it was.

Gary and Teddy and I went out to dinner one night at the Princessa Marina, a seafood restaurant. I had never eaten lobster before, and Gary wanted me to try it. We got there early and were almost the only ones in there.

I had some shrimp and a glass of wine. Gary ordered lobster and he insisted that I try it. It was very rich, and I preferred my shrimp, but Gary insisted that I eat some. The lobster was just okay, according to Gary. He was from the USA and he said the lobster was better there.

When dinner was over we all took a taxi back to the middle of town. Gary doesn't drink and goes to bed early, so he left to take the bus home to his apartment. It was a Wednesday night and I asked Teddy if he wanted to go with me to the Rosa de Desamparados, a nice bar in my neighborhood. He said sure, and off we went.

When we got there it was still pretty early, maybe around nine. There were a few people I knew there. Sitting at the table in front of my favorite table were my two downstairs neighbors, Elena and Pablo. My granddaughter Graciela was babysitting their little girl. They seemed to be having a good time. Teddy and I sat at my favorite table in the back near the kitchen, and I noticed my stomach wasn't feeling very good. The lobster I had eaten wasn't sitting well. Teddy and I both ordered a beer and I hoped that mine would settle my stomach.

The beer didn't do me any good, and I went into the ladies room to vomit. I was hoping that was all I needed, but I still felt sick afterward. By this time Pablo and Elena were sitting at the table. Pablo does a lot of cocaine and when he's doing it he can't stop talking. Teddy was doing his best to be polite but the music in the bar was loud and he doesn't always understand when people talk fast to him in Spanish. It didn't matter to Pablo whether Teddy understood, he was just talking because of the drug.

I told Teddy I was sorry, but I felt horrible and wanted to just go home. He told me he would go with me but I told him no, I just wanted to go alone, be alone. He knows better than to argue with me, so he said okay, he would finish his beer and go home himself, which he did.

When I got back to my apartment, I was upset to find the baby asleep in the bedroom and Graciela nowhere around. I was angry with her for leaving the baby alone, and my stomach felt horrible. I went into the bathroom, got sick, and when I was cleaned up, I called Graciela to scold her for leaving the baby alone. She was about a block away with one of her "boyfriends," a drug dealer named Oscar. Oscar was quite a bit older, in his thirties at least, and I didn't like Graciela being involved with an older man like that, especially a drug dealer. But one good thing was that he didn't let her do drugs or get drunk. I was grateful for that.

Elena and Pablo came home, and I told them that Graciela just left when I got home because the baby was asleep. I was still getting sick when my phone rang and it was my friend, Carmela. She wanted to come over but I was still getting sick so I told the Elena to talk to her, tell her I was too sick to talk. Carmela came over anyway. She brought me some soup from a Chinese place, but I couldn't eat it. Elena had gone downstairs with the baby by then but Pablo was still in my apartment, sitting on the bed talking to me and Carmela. Carmela got a call on her phone, some sort of problem back at her place, so she left. I was sitting on the bed with Pablo and he was snorting coke and talking. I was still feeling pretty bad but I didn't know how to get rid of Pablo.

It was only a few minutes later when Carmela called again to say that everything was okay at her place. But while I was on the phone with her, Pablo and I heard a couple of gunshots outside. This worried me a lot because Graciela was up the street at Oscar's and I thought maybe something had happened there. The guys that worked for Oscar had guns. I was still very weak, so I asked Pablo to go up the street and see what was going on and tell me if the shots were from Oscar's place. Carmela heard all this and told me she was coming right over. I asked her to bring me some rice and beans, something easy on my stomach. I was hungry now because my stomach was empty after vomiting so much.

So Pablo put on a pair of Graciela's sandals and walked up the street. He didn't even have a shirt on. When he came back he said not to worry, that it was somebody else up near the corner, not anybody from Oscar's. When Pablo came back, he said Oscar wanted to talk to me. I asked Pablo to go tell Oscar that I was grateful that he was keeping Graciela out of trouble, but I was just too sick to come up and talk. Pablo said that Oscar was outside and could I just come out on the balcony and talk to him for a little while? I wasn't in the mood, but I didn't want any trouble with Oscar. Nobody did. So I went out on the balcony. Oscar was standing down below at the foot of the stairs. I went out and thanked him for keeping Graciela out of trouble, and keeping her from doing drugs.

One of the reasons I hadn't wanted to talk to Oscar was that he had been angry at me because of something that happened a month or two before. Graciela was fooling around with two boyfriends back then, both of them drug dealers. She was seeing Oscar and she was also seeing José, the eighteen year old that caused Valeria to throw her out of the house.

What happened was I came home one afternoon and found Graciela back in the bedroom with José, smoking mota. Well, I was trying to keep Graciela out of trouble, but living where we live there's no way I can keep her from doing drugs if that's what she wants to do. All I tried to do keep her away from the worst drugs and if she was going to do something I asked her not to do it behind my back. I'm no nun; I like my mota and a little coca [cocaine] too. I like to drink beer and sometimes something stronger. But I'm not fifteen years old and I know what I'm doing.

I was angry with Graciela for letting the younger boyfriend in her room to smoke mota. This wasn't the first time I had trouble with the José. He had gotten into some sort of fight with my mother, God knows why, but he had caused problems for me before. So José was in the bedroom with Graciela when Oscar showed up asking for Graciela. I knew there could be some big trouble if Oscar caught Graciela and José together. Graciela came out and the left José in the bedroom. She knew what could happen if Oscar caught her in the bedroom alone with José. She came down the stairs to talk to Oscar. She wanted to stop him from coming in, of course, so she left to go up to Oscar's place and left me to tell José. José knew that Oscar was outside, so he was glad to get out without Oscar knowing.

I was angry with Graciela, and as she was leaving I told her I was fed up and couldn't go on like this. I told her I was going to talk to Valeria and that I didn't want to be involved in any more of her problems. I wanted to get out of there in case of trouble so I went up to the pulperia [a small grocery store, sometimes just run from somebody's front room]. Oscar took this as an insult to him, though he wasn't the reason I was angry. I was angry at Graciela.

Anyway, Graciela left with Oscar that day and eventually Oscar found out why I was so angry with her and he wasn't angry with me any more, but he wanted to talk to me. I went out on the balcony and told him I was sorry if he felt offended but I explained that there was another man in Graciela's room and I didn't want to be in the middle of all that trouble. Oscar said that he was angry at first because he thought I meant he was the problem, but now he understood. Graciela was back at his place by that time, sleeping. He gave her something to help her sleep, and I thanked him for that.

While we were talking, one of his "employees" came up and asked me for a cigarette. I told him yeah, I had a cigarette but I would bring it down to him because we were talking outside and it was three in the morning and I didn't want to bother the neighbors. My mother lives below, and my sister Pati lives next door. I went downstairs and we were talking at the foot of the stairs that go up to my apartment. While we were talking, Carmela called me again and said she was going to bring me something else to eat, and she asked me if I had any guaro or beer, and I told her no, it was three in the morning and everything was closed. Oscar heard me and told me he could get guaro and beer because he had his own little pulperia. So Carmela came over and Oscar came back with a bottle of Johnny Walker, a six pack of beer, some ginger ale, some crackers and two packs of cigarettes. I still didn't feel so good, but now there was a party going on in my place whether I liked it or not. Pablo was still there, and just a little while later three of Oscar's "employees" showed up, and before I knew it there were seven people drinking and talking in my little place and it was getting near four in the morning. It was insane. They were snorting coke, smoking pot, drinking, and some of them were doing ketamine. I wanted them all to leave so I could rest and recuperate from being sick, but I didn't want any trouble with Oscar.

The party went on until finally I took Carmela aside and told her I was exhausted and afraid the party was getting out of hand. I knew that Oscar and his "employees" all had guns and they were getting really fucked up. This was my apartment and my family all lived nearby. I told Carmela I was afraid something bad might happen. I felt sick and I was tired. Could we go to her place? That was the only way I could see that we could get all those guys out of my apartment. Carmela was a drug dealer too, but at least there wouldn't be all these guys with guns and everything. So we told everybody we were leaving. Since it was my place, they all left and went off somewhere else to continue the party. I was glad to get out of there because I had a bad feeling something bad was going to happen and I didn't want it to happen in my place.

The sun was already up when we got to Carmela's place. I was very tired from being sick and up so late, and I went right to sleep. When I finally woke up the next afternoon about two, I was worried about Graciela. I remembered what was going on the night before and I was worried. I was still in the same clothes. I hurried outside and got a taxi back to my place.

I went inside and Graciela was there, but she was white as a sheet. It was obvious that something was wrong. I asked her what happened. At first she said nothing happened. I asked her again and she said nothing, she had to go. She left and headed up the street to where Oscar lived. It was only a few minutes later when I heard a gunshot. It sounded like it might have come from Oscar's house, and Graciela was there, so I ran up there to see what had happened. The door to Oscar's place was open and I saw Graciela just inside. "Come here! Come here!" she told me. I went inside and saw several men gathered together talking very seriously.

I asked Graciela "What happened?"

"Mami, they just shot a man here!"

"Graciela, I don't believe it!"

"Mami, it's true, I saw him lying on the floor. He was moaning "Help me!" but I couldn't do anything, somebody might shoot me too!"

She pointed around the corner of the room and there was the man on the floor, bleeding. I told Graciela we needed to get out of there but Oscar's men wouldn't let us leave. They were afraid we'd call the police. We promised not to say anything but they told us we had to stay. They told us they weren't going to do anything to us, harm us, but they couldn't let us leave. The guy who was shot was still alive. They got a sheet, put him in it and carried him out to a car. There is a clinic in Desamparados and they drove him close by there and took him out and put him in a corner of the parking lot where nobody could see him. There was a beggar who "worked" the parking lot, "guarding" cars and getting tips once in a while worth a quarter maybe. One of the Oscar's men told the beggar there was a man over in the corner of the lot, and gave him 5000 colones [the equivalent of ten dollars] to go tell somebody inside that he just found the guy there bleeding and not to say anything about who told him. Once they had given the beggar the money, they drove away.

All the while this was going on, Graciela and I weren't allowed to leave Oscar's place. We weren't exactly prisoners, but they didn't want to take any chances that we'd say anything to anybody. The police came and were sniffing around after the shots were fired, but there wasn't any body or any evidence of anything that went on. Oscar had his "employees" clean up all the blood so that nobody would ever suspect that anybody had been shot inside his house.

They finally let us go when everything had finally calmed down enough and the worst had passed. They told us we had better not tell the police or anybody. They didn't have to worry about that!

The guy that was shot was hurt pretty badly, but he was smart enough not to tell anybody who shot him. His mother knew what happened and she was upset. But she was a crack addict they bought her off with some crack and a little money. She wasn't going to be a problem.

It was all so stupid, so pointless. My bad feeling turned out to be right. What can you expect from a bunch of fucked up guys with guns? Two of them got into an argument about who was going to get the last dose of ketamine and it ended with one guy shooting the other guy. Imagine, shooting someone for a fucking dose of ketamine!

MOVING

I can't count the number of times I've moved and the number of different places I have lived in the last few years. I usually stay in or around Desamparados. Right now I am splitting my time between San José with a gringo and Desamparados, where I have a room upstairs from my mother. I was living with the gringo full time for a while, but I really need my own space. He doesn't like me watching television and I get bored without it. I moved in with him to get away from the couple of Nicaraguans that my mother rented one of the upstairs rooms to. They were always fighting and hogging the bathroom. They finally moved out and I could move back in but my gringo helps me out a little with money and it's convenient living downtown when I want to work or party there.

PATI

When I was with Milena, we lived for almost a year and a half with my sister Pati. Patricia has always been good to me, but the place was run down and had rats and cockroaches all over. I'm very fastidious, and it bothered me a lot. It was hard for me to sleep hearing the rats running around.

One time I was having sex with Milena during a rainstorm. We were so carried away that we didn't notice the water flooding into our little room. Finally my sister shouted "Magdalena, get out of the room, we're being flooded!" And we looked down and the water was almost up to the edge of the bed. The drains outside were full of garbage and they backed up. That's what caused the flood.

One day while I was getting ready to go out to work, I stepped on a rat and killed it. Just the day before I smelled something awful and found a dead rat in the bathroom. It was gigantic. I hate dirt and I hate messes. I was always cleaning my room with Clorox and disinfectant but it was never enough. I would open the refrigerator and there would be cockroaches inside. It was really hard on me to live in that sort of environment. My family isn't like me. Living like that doesn't bother them like it does me. I finally had to move.

After Pati's, I split up from Milena and went to live for a little while with my friend Maria José. I've known her since Hotel El Jardin. She has a pretty face but she's let her body go and doesn't make much money lately. We get along fine but she's not responsible and didn't pay her fair share. I ended up spending money so her kids had something to eat. I have my own problems and she should support her own children. When I had enough of that, I went to live with my brother Danilo in a nice place he had found. Danilo is quite a bit younger and his father is Juan. The apartment was only a couple of hundred meters from the old Rosa de Desamparados and it was practically new. It wasn't all that big, but it was big enough for the two of us. That situation didn't last long, though. My brother isn't very responsible and didn't have his part of the rent money when the second month came around. By that time Anayeti had been staying there with my brother, and she took over the room, and was going to pay half the rent. But she wasn't any more responsible than Danilo. Even when she had money she spent it on drugs and alcohol, not rent or utilities. We finally had to give the place up. She moved back in with her oldest daughter and that's when I moved in with Graciela and the rest for a little while.

It's too bad I couldn't keep that place. It was nice. I remember having a fun party there for my 45th birthday. There were lots of neighbors and friends and even a couple of gringos who brought beer and guaro. It's good they came because it wouldn't have been all that much of a party otherwise. Teddy was one of the gringos and the other was Art, an older guy, about seventy. It was the last time I saw Art. He lived alone in his own apartment a few kilometers away. I didn't hear from him for a few months, and I was shocked when somebody told me he was dead. It was really sad how they found him. He died alone and it wasn't until his body began to smell and the neighbors complained to the landlord. He was a nice man, and it's sad how he died all alone, and nobody even knew.

Aptos Fernando

After I gave up the apartment with Yeti, I moved in with Gloriana for a little while, but not for long. Marco Two doesn't like it when I drink and it's just part of my job. I didn't like living with them anyway. The kids are little brats and it was impossible to sleep. Once I had enough money, I moved back into an apartment near where Andrea, my son's wife, was living.

Milena moved in with me again, and she was working at the time, so we could afford to live there. But Andrea was always asking me for money. I really couldn't spare much, if anything. Milena and I were barely getting by ourselves. Andrea had two daughters by then and her husband, Alan was in prison. She had to understand they were her responsibility, not mine. She's the one who had two babies while her husband was in prison! It wasn't my idea. It made me sad that I couldn't help them, but I couldn't. When she needed to go out, to go to the clinic or shop or look for work I watched her babies. But it was hard because I couldn't sleep when I had to watch them. Sometimes I was up late the night before and I would have to watch them early in the morning. I tried to help but it was very rough on me. All this shouldn't have been my problem.

Since my son went to prison my life has been a disaster. I have to think of my granddaughters, I have to get money for Alan, I have to pay for my apartment, I have to pay for food... Maybe I need to find a boyfriend or girlfriend to help me straighten out my situation, but I don't want to. I don't want to live with anybody. I don't want to have to explain where I go, what I do or don't do to anybody. It's terrible. I'd like to find a job so I could live a normal life. I would love a steady salary. But there aren't many things I can do. I never went to school at all, and I'm forty-eight years old. I look younger but when they ask for my ID they look at my age and don't want to hire me. They don't want older people.

LANDLORD WHO DIDN'T PAY ELECTRIC

When Milena and I broke up again, I got a cheaper place for just myself in Desamparados. I was only there for a few months when I started having problems with the landlord. He didn't pay the electric bill and I was without electricity. Then the water was cut off. I wasn't going to pay the rent if there was no water or electricity. But the landlord wanted his rent money anyhow. Then he decided he wanted me out, but I had no place to go and I didn't have enough to get a new place. I heard from one of the neighbors that he was going to pay a couple of guys to steal everything I had out of my place if as soon as I left the house unguarded.

Gloriana was living just a few doors away, and I asked her to please stay in the house while I went into San José to make a little money. She didn't want to, I could tell, but she agreed to stay for a few hours. I barely got downtown when she called to say her husband had come home and told her he didn't want her in my apartment. So she said she was going to go back home. I was upset, of course. But I came back home because I was afraid somebody would steal all my things.

It was bad enough that I didn't have any money, but then I got sick. I had a fever and I ached all over. So I sat there in the dark, just crying, with no money, nothing to eat, and both my daughters living close by. I tried calling Gloriana to see if she would lend me a little money so I could buy something to eat, some rice and beans, a sandwich, some bread, just something because I didn't have anything. I would pay her back when I was able, but she didn't answer the phone and didn't answer any of the messages I left for her. I felt so alone. I prayed to God to give me the strength to carry on. I felt abandoned by my daughters. When they want something they are right there but when I'm too sick and poor to even buy a loaf of bread they are nowhere to be found. I was sick and alone in that dark apartment for three days and do you think either one of them bothered to come and see how I was? After all I did for them for so many years. They don't care about me. It's not right. I pray to God to help me stay alive. I'm not getting any younger.

If it wasn't for my friends I would have died of hunger or pneumonia a long time ago. My family sure wouldn't have saved me. But when something happens to them... they come to me, running. When Gloriana was fighting with Marco Two and he threatened her with a pistol, she ran to me with her four brats and stayed in my tiny little apartment for two weeks! But when I need something, forget it. More times than I can count I have needed a place to stay but no, that's just not possible she tells me. It's the same with Valeria. They both put their partners first. I was never that way. I put my children in front of my husband or boyfriends or girlfriends. I would never let anybody touch my children, but Marco Two beats Gloriana's children and it got bad enough where the neighbors called the social services and reported them. I never let anybody touch my children. Never!

And my son is no better. He is in jail and he expects me to bring him food on visitor's day and bring him money so he can buy some cigarettes and candy and such. But he doesn't worry that maybe I'm sick and don't have any money to buy food for myself. I suppose it's my fault that they take advantage of me. I can't just tell them "no" when they need me, but they sure don't care about me. If I'm sick they don't care if I live or die. I'm very tired of life. Very tired.

I finally moved back upstairs from my mother and Juan after the problems I had with that landlord. On Sundays I usually go visit my son in prison, and I usually go early. But one Sunday I was sleeping later because he had arranged for some girl to come have sex with him, so I was going to visit later. My room is upstairs from my mother's, where my brother Danilo was staying. I was still in bed at about eight that Sunday when I heard three cars pull up really fast in front of the house. I got up in a hurry and I heard very loud knocking on my mother's door.

So I went out on the balcony and looked down and there were three police cars outside, with their lights flashing. I looked down and I saw the police were forcing the door open with a crowbar. In a minute or so I saw the police taking away my brother Danilo in handcuffs. So I had two brothers and a son in jail. Rodrigo had been in jail for selling drugs to minors and he would be in a long time. And now Danilo was in jail too. They arrested him for not paying child support. He told me that last week paid the mother $110 and she told him she'd sign later a receipt later, but she went and filed charges with the police instead. So the police came and took him to jail. At least that's Danilo' story.

Poor Danilo. They were going to keep him in jail for six months. He owed $400 so he got six months. My mother finally got the money together to get him out. She pawned her television and some other things. She would never have done that for me. Maybe it's because Danilo is Juan's son. I just know she never did anything for me when I was young.

FUN WITH JENNI

I was in the Arenal Bar with Jenni, but there wasn't anything there, nobody looking for company, so Jenni said "Let's walk down to Joe B's, maybe there's some business there." I told her I was tired and didn't want to walk but I finally agreed and off we went. I was wearing a very sexy dress, as usual when I am working. When we got out in front of the Presidente Hotel I ran into a man I knew, a sweet man who was headed to Joe B's to see his favorite bartender. We talked for a minute and he kissed me on the cheek when he left. While he was talking to me there was another man watching us. Jenni whispered to me that the other man was staring at my butt. That was fine with me. So Jenni asked him if he wanted to party with us both, if he wanted two girls. He didn't say anything, just smiled. I was embarrassed and I grabbed Jenni and we walked down to Joe B's.

When we got to Joe B's I saw a lot of people I knew and I was saying hello, kissing them on the cheek when I looked back and saw the man from in front of the Presidente. He said "Please, can I talk to you?" I told him certainly, that I noticed he was looking at my butt. He laughed and said yes, I had a very cute butt. He offered to buy me a beer and I said sure and asked him to buy one for Jenni too, which he did. He asked me my name and how old I was. I asked him how old he thought I was. He said 36. I said I was 37 (I'm 48!). "You close! You close!" I told him.

"Are you available tonight?" he asked.

"Yes, sure," I answered.

"How much do you charge?"

"I don't know, how much will you pay?"

He said "$40 each."

I said "Let's go, that's fine," and we left together for his apartment. We spent about 2 hours together and he was very affectionate, like he was my boyfriend.

He called me up about a week later and told me "Magdalena, I have a bunch of other interesting things for you." Now the time before he had a big collection of vibrators and sex toys, so I couldn't imagine what else he might have, but he asked me if I could come and I told him sure. So I went to his apartment and we talked for a while and had a beer. Then he took me over to the bed and there were handcuffs on the bed! Uh Oh! That scared me. They are going to kill me! I told him no, I wasn't going to do that. I told him that I had done a lot of things but I didn't want him to hurt me. He said, "No, no, I'm not going to hurt you, that's not what I want." So I told him okay but he couldn't put the cuffs on me tight, that I wanted to be able to free my hands if I needed to. So he said okay but he tried to put them on tight anyway. But I'm skinny and I knew that I could get my hands loose if I had to, but he didn't know that.

So he fastened my hands and feet, and he put a ball gag in my mouth. And he got out his vibrators and I had like 15 orgasms! Finally I couldn't do any more, I was worn out. So he said okay, MY TURN! Okay, I said, and I put the cuffs on nice and tight.

Then he said, okay, start with the little vibrator up my anus. When I get used to it put the bigger one there, but not the really big one. Well, I was feeling naughty and I put the big one in there. At first he was going "Ow, ow" but I could tell he was loving it, he was very turned on. His being turned on turned ME on one more time so while I was sucking him I was using one of his vibrators on myself. It didn't take long until we both came, very strong. My God, what a night!

INTERVIEW WITH PATRICIA

[I am the oldest in the family, Magdalena was the second. I didn't live with my mother most of the time. I was raised by my mother's sister, who was also very poor but she wasn't an alcoholic. But we lived very close, and I was in the house with Magdalena, Rodrigo and Yorleny pretty often. Because I was the oldest I would be in charge of my younger brother and sisters. Before she met Juan, my mother would go out a lot to the cantinas and we would have to try to find something to eat. We would all go begging at the mercado [farmer's market] and we usually got enough to make some soup, at least.

I was lucky that I didn't live with them when Juan moved in. I didn't have the same problem with him that Magdalena and Yorleny did, mostly because I could always go to my aunt's place to get away. He did try to touch me but I would just go.

My aunt was able to keep me in school until the fifth grade. I was probably thirteen at the time. I got married at fourteen, mostly to get away from the house. My husband had a job, nothing great, but we could eat and we stayed together a long time, enough to have five children together. I'm the only one of my mother's children whose children all had the same father. Magdalena's three children all have different fathers. Yorleny is a lesbian and has no children. Magdalena's daughters both have children by different fathers. I'm the only one with just one father to all my children.

I never worked as a prostitute. I was married quite a while, and we were able to get by. And I was never as pretty and lively as my sister, so I don't think I would have made much money. But I get along now like a lot of people I know. I clean houses or do laundry sometimes and I sell small amounts of cocaine and mota as well, enough to get by usually. My children help me if they can and I am doing better than when I was a little girl. I am poor and life isn't always easy, but I still enjoy myself. I have my family and we mostly get along pretty well.

I get along better with my children than Magdalena does with her daughters. She was a better mother to them than our mother was to us, but I know that both Gloriana and Valeria feel like they were neglected. They didn't go without food or clothes or a place to sleep, but they didn't get much attention from their mother, and they have both told me they felt neglected by her. Right now Valeria isn't talking to Magdalena at all. Gloriana gets along better with her, but Marco Two doesn't approve of Magdalena's drinking and they aren't on good terms.

Gloriana separated from Marco two a few times, but they always get back together. Gloriana has five children now, two by Marco Two. Rachel, her oldest, is twelve now and nobody knows where the father is. Her second was a boy she named after her brother, Alan. The father was a boy from the neighborhood, but he doesn't give her anything for support. He just got her pregnant. Her third was a girl by her first husband, named Marco. She left the first Marco for another man named Marco and has had two children by him. The first Marco supported the whole family *when they were together, and gave her money to support their daughter after they split up. He is a very nice man, very responsible, but he just wasn't passionate enough for Gloriana. So she went with the second Marco and he turned out to be very violent and beats her and her first three children. The first Marco took his daughter to live with him when he heard.*

Valeria is a hard worker and takes care of herself. She and Magdalena don't get along. They never did. Valeria thinks Magdalena was a bad mother. Magdalena doesn't like that, and thinks Valeria has been a bad mother to Graciela. Magdalena has taken Graciela in when Valeria threw her out. I think Magdalena would forgive her daughter but Valeria is pretty hard and not a forgiving person. I think it's a shame, but nobody's going to change how they are.]

ATTEMPTED RAPE AND SHOOTING

Sometimes my work gets really dangerous. It was about two years ago, and I was in the Arenal Bar with a couple of gringos and a friend around 2 AM, which was closing time. The gringos went home and my friend and I decided to walk over to the Cozumel Club, which is open till past dawn. I usually go home before 11 when the last bus leaves but I still needed about $30 more to pay my rent, which was due the next day.

As we were walking over, a VW Microbus was following us, and there was a guy inside who was calling out to me. I asked him what he wanted and he said he wanted to go with me, that I was very pretty, and he wanted have sex with me. My friends went inside and I stayed outside to talk to the guy. But all the while we were talking I could tell he was playing with himself. I thought that was vulgar and weird, and maybe he would be dangerous.

While I was talking to him another guy came up on a small motorcycle and started to talk to me. I could tell by the way he talked he was a Tico. I don't like going out with Ticos, and I almost never do. But I needed the money. The guy on the motorcycle wanted me to go with him to a hotel but I told him I was afraid of motorcycles because I had been in an accident once. He told me not to worry, that he would drive very slowly and carefully and if I got scared he would let me off and pay for a taxi for me. He spoke very gently to me and politely. I told him I needed to go to the bathroom, and went inside and stayed for about 10 minutes. I was almost hoping he would lose patience and leave. But when I finally came out he was still there, so I agreed to go with him. We drove off towards San Sebastian where he said there was a hotel he knew. This was also close to my home so I agreed and got on the motorcycle. He only had the one helmet, which he wore, and none for me. I was afraid but as I have said, I needed the money.

We went towards San Sebastian but when we were nearby he turned off onto a side street. I asked him why he was turning and he said he had to pee. He drove to a little park. There was nobody around. He stopped the motorcycle and got off, and turned his back to me. Suddenly, he turned around and I saw he had a pistol in his hand, which he put it up to my head. I yelled at him "What are you doing?" and he pushed me and yelled at me "Shut up and do everything I say."

Well, when I saw the pistol I lost control. I shouted back "Go ahead and kill me, you bastard. My life is shit anyway!" and I ran up to him. He pushed me away and shot me twice, once just grazing my neck and the second into my forehead. Thank heaven it was only a pellet gun, or I would be dead now. As it was I was bleeding and crazy with rage. I guess this must have scared him. It definitely hadn't gone as he planned. Anyway, he hopped on his motorcycle and sped off. It's funny to think of it now. He expected to scare me and I ended up scaring HIM.

My phone wasn't working but I found a public phone and I called my sister Pati, collect. She said she was coming to get me, along with her son. They were almost there when they saw a police car that had pulled over a car with some guys inside. My sister told them that I had been shot, and would they please take her to help me. They told her no, they were in the middle of an arrest. She knew this was a lie because the police car wasn't from that area. The cops were just shaking down the guy in the car for a bribe.

When she got where I was and saw how much I was bleeding she was very afraid, and we went back past the police car. They were still in the same place, and so was the other car. My sister yelled at the police "Look at my sister, she's bleeding and all you want to do is get a bribe from this guy!" My nephew took some photos with his phone of the police car to report them, but the police grabbed his phone and wouldn't give it back. Great police we have here.

We all walked back to my sister's house, where she cleaned me up and stopped the bleeding. I should have gone to the clinic but I don't have insurance and I didn't have the money to pay anybody. People have told me they would have had to treat me because it was an emergency, but I wasn't thinking clearly and anyway, I am afraid of hospitals.

The result was that I had the pellet inside the skin above my eyebrow for over a month. I was starting to get headaches and feeling worse and worse. I was scared, but I'm afraid of doctors and hospitals. Finally, my friend Teddy had to take me by the hand and almost drag me to see a doctor. I was petrified but Teddy was firm and paid for everything and the doctor took out the pellet. After the incision healed I felt okay again, but it was very scary for me. I was shaking. It only hurt a little, thank God.

ANAYETI STORY

There's always some kind of drama going on around me. One Wednesday night about a year ago I was out with Teddy again in the Rosa de Desamparados. It was getting to be around midnight and Teddy was feeling a little drunk so he decided to go home. Anayeti was in the bar that night and she was fighting with her ex boyfriend. She wanted to break up with him but he didn't want to and he was making it hard on her.

I told her I didn't want that shit going on at my table, so they went outside. He finally left and she came back inside. She had a little mota and a little guaro, so we decided to go to her apartment to party a little more. So we were drinking, smoking and doing a little cocaine, and just talking about the usual stuff, problems with boyfriend and girlfriends, sharing gossip.

Her apartment is on the second floor but she has her own stairs that go up on the outside, maybe fifteen stairs. Anyway, after a couple of hours we heard footsteps coming up the stairs. We could see out the window and it was Giovanni, the ex boyfriend. He started pounding on the door. I told Anayeti not to open the door, it was her ex and he was drunk and drugged and crazy and was going to cause problems. I knew if she let him in that we were all going to get involved and nobody needs that kind of trouble. Finally he gave up and we heard him walk down the stairs. Great, we thought. He's gone. That's what we thought.

We didn't think there was any way Giovanni could get in other than through the front door because she lived on the second floor and there was only the one set of stairs and the one door. But just a minute or two later we heard some strange noise outside of her bedroom, and we realized that Giovanni had climbed up on the roof of the house next door. Then we heard a crash and the sound of breaking glass. He had broken into her bedroom by breaking the window. It was incredible how he got up there... like a cat! It was even more amazing considering he was drunk. I knew it was Giovanni and told Anayeti to run away, but she didn't and just stood in the doorway at the top of the steps. I went into the bedroom and told him she had left, but he didn't believe me and went to look in the bathroom.

By now Anayeti was halfway down the stairs and I yelled at her to run, but she didn't run and Giovanni caught up with her on the stairs and grabbed her by the hair. I was the one closest to them so I started running down the stairs because I wasn't going to let him beat up on her. But as I was running down the stairs one of my heels caught in the stairs and I slipped and fell down the stairs on my butt, boom boom boom, like in a cartoon. I'm sure it looked funny but it hurt like hell, and I could barely walk for about two weeks.

So there I was down at the bottom of the stairs, not really able to move, and by this time everybody in the house below had come out and were beating on Giovanni. I told them "Call the police! Call the police!" but they didn't want to do that and they just let him hobble off.

I spent the night at Anayeti's because I was too sore to go home. I was still trying to recuperate when I heard an ambulance and the police sirens. They were there because Giovanni had stabbed himself in the stomach with a knife, trying to kill himself. Ay ay ay! What a world!

DESAMPARADOS STORY - THE CRAZY GIRL

It was only a few weeks after Giovanni tried to kill himself with a knife that I was in the Flor again, and I saw this girl I know, Analia. I've known her for quite a few years and she's always had problems. She had her two children taken away from her by Child Services because she was doing a lot of cocaine and drinking too much. About a year ago somebody brought me a newspaper and there a story about a girl who shot herself in the stomach at a motel, and there was Analia's name and photo. She later told me she had gone to a motel with a man she met, but she had been doing a lot of cocaine and drinking. Once they were in the room, the man went into the bathroom. He had a pistol with him that he left on the table and while he was in the bathroom Analia took the pistol and shot herself twice in the stomach. They took her to the hospital and she lived, though it was close.

It was about midnight and I was ready to go home. I lived close by, and Analia came over to my table and asked me if she could come over to my apartment to do a little cocaine since it was a bad idea to do it in the bar. She said she had some mota I could smoke if she could come over. Well, I like mota and I didn't have any, so I told her okay, but that I wasn't going to stay up all night with her. She said fine, she would be over in just a little while, so I left.

I waited until two and she still hadn't shown up, so I went to bed. It was about four in the morning when she woke me up, knocking on my door. I had been sleeping and I was angry with her for being so late and waking me up. She said she was sorry and talked me into letting her inside. She gave me a joint and I smoked it while she did a couple of lines of cocaine. It was late and I fell back asleep. When I got up about eight the next morning, she was still awake, still doing cocaine and she looked pretty bad. I told her I was going to walk over to the little store and get us something to eat for breakfast. When I got back, she was lying on my bed and the front of her dress was soaked with blood and there was a knife with blood on it lying beside her. I was afraid, but just like before, when I get afraid I get angry. I was shouting at her, asking her what the hell she thought she was doing. She didn't say anything, but grabbed the knife and stabbed herself again twice! I called my sister Pati. I knew where her brothers lived and I would have gone and got them, but I didn't want to leave her alone, who knows what she would have done. So Pati came to stay with Analia while I went to get her brothers. When they saw Analia, they were angry with ME, as if it was MY fault their sister had stabbed herself!

They finally took her away and I could relax. I'll never understand people who want to hurt themselves like that. Never.

PINCHE GRINGOS

I've had a lot of clients over the years. When I was in my best years I met some wonderful men, kind and generous. Most of my clients were pretty forgettable though, and I forgot them! And then there are the ones I would like to forget, the dick faces.

Some men just have no class. They think because we're prostitutes it's alright to treat us like shit. Some are cheap, some are insulting, and some are even violent. There were a few in the New York Bar that nobody wanted to go with. One of them was a guy that called himself "Buck." He was very cocky. Even the other gringos thought he was an ass. I didn't pay him much attention at first because business was still fairly good for me back then. There were more gringos back then and I really didn't get to know all that many of them very well because most of the time they just wanted a quick blow job, 20 minutes for $20, and we didn't fuck, just a quick blow job. We would usually just go around the corner to the Hotel Asia or if they had a car I'd blow the guy in the car. Then I'd go back in the bar and party a little and if I was lucky maybe get another customer or two even. I didn't get to know many of the men there mainly because it was just quickies like that, and I wasn't interested in Buck because he was loud and vulgar, always groping the girls, not treating them with respect.

But over time I did get to know him and when I was in a good mood and joking around it didn't really bother me if he wanted to grab my butt. Finally, there was one night when I was low on money and he was the only potential customer in the bar. Anyway, he was staying at the Morazan, just up the street, and we left for his room. He was drunk, like he usually was, and he couldn't finish. I was there with him, blowing him, blowing him but he just couldn't get the job done. Finally, after a half hour of this, I told him my mouth was getting tired and I couldn't keep going. He got angry and told me he wasn't going to pay me because he didn't come. I said it wasn't my fault, I had tried my best. I always wanted my clients to be happy with me when they left, to be satisfied, because I didn't want them telling other gringos that I was no good. But he was just too drunk to come. He thought about it a second and said I was right, it wasn't my fault and he gave me $25, although he had agreed to pay me $40. It wasn't what he promised but it was better than nothing, and he told me that tomorrow night he wanted to see me when he wasn't drinking so much and I said okay. Like other times when I did something I didn't really want to do, it was because I really needed the money.

So I was there the next night and he was there too, but he was with another girl. I asked him why he was with another girl and he told me not to worry, he was going to take her back to his room to give her some money and then he would come back to the bar for me. I didn't believe him, I thought he would go have sex with her and wouldn't come back to the bar, but about an hour later he came back and we went to his hotel room. This time he was nice and quick, and he gave me $30 and that was that. He still didn't give me the $40 he promised the first night. Times were tough and he was a steady customer, so for about two months I would see him maybe twice a week. Sometimes, if I fell asleep and spent the night he'd give me $60, otherwise if we spent 2 hours together he'd give me $40. That was cheap enough, but I finally stopped going with him because he decided he was only going to pay $20 for all night. It's just not worth it. I don't like him and I don't like being with him. He wants to have sex all night, grope me all night long off and on, and then have sex again in the morning. I'm not that old and ugly that I have to put up with all that for just $20.

When I first met him he was new to Costa Rica. He wasn't paying a lot but he was at least paying what was reasonable. But the longer he's been here the cheaper he's gotten. Now he just looks for the cheapest girl he can find, the most desperate. I helped him out one time to find a new apartment, cheaper than what he had. After spending an hour helping him out, I asked him if he would give me a little money for my granddaughter's birthday so I could buy some balloons and a piñata, but he said no, he didn't have any money, which is bullshit. He's just a cheap pig. That did it for me. I don't care how hard up I get; I'm not going to waste my time with that cheap dick face. He wants me to spend all night with him listening to him talk about how great he is when he's not molesting me, all for $20 all night. It's not like he doesn't have the money. He showed me pictures of his sons and they are both rich and both very handsome as well. He's not poor; he's just a cheap bastard. No more Buck for me. I'll go hungry first.

I've had a few clients who have tried to beat me up or hurt me, even shoot me. I even had one guy try to push me off a 5th floor balcony. It was another cheap gringo. I was walking to the New York bar on my way to work one night through Parque Central and this man saw me and he went "psst, psst" at me. Well, work is work so I turned around and said hello to him, and I asked him if he spoke Spanish. He said he spoke a little but he didn't want to talk he wanted to do something with me. I asked him what he had in mind. He said he wanted my company, wanted to take some pictures. He said that I looked and walked very sexy. Since we were in the park, I could have been a secretary for all he knew.

I asked him what he wanted me to do. He told me we could talk about that in his apartment. I said fine, we could talk about that in his apartment but I was working and I wasn't going to go with him without getting paid. He said fine, fine, we'd talk about all that in his apartment. I told him fine, but I needed money, that was my job and he said okay, he'd pay me some money and give me some perfumes, because that's what he did, sold perfume. So I thought that maybe I would be able to sell the perfume or keep it but since it was the first client of the day, I agreed to go. It's a sort of superstition with some of us that you shouldn't turn down the first customer because it's bad luck and you won't get anything else. So I agreed to go with him and we took a taxi to his apartment.

When we got there he got me a beer and got one for himself. So we were in the living room and he said "take off your clothes" and I said "Take it easy, what's the hurry? Can I trust you?" and he told me he was a good person and I could trust him, so I took off my clothes and we had sex. After we were done and I had done what he wanted, I told him I had to go, and I needed him to pay me. When I said that, he got angry. "I told you I didn't have any money!" he said. "That's not true," I told him. "You said you'd pay me a little money and give me some perfume. I need some money, at least $10. I can't eat perfume!" He told me I could take some perfume, but he wasn't going to give me any money. So I got really mad and told him I was going to call the police.

His apartment was somewhere in the center of San José, I don't remember exactly where, but I do remember we were on the 5th floor and there was a balcony. So when I told him I was going to call the police he grabbed me by the throat and took me over to the balcony and told me he would throw me off if I tried to call the police. I could take the perfume and leave, or leave with nothing, but he wasn't going to pay me and if I tried to call the police he'd throw me off the balcony. I was pretty scared, you can imagine, so I told him I'd take the perfume and wouldn't call the police. He made me take the chip out of my phone so I couldn't call. So I took what perfume I could and left in a hurry. Another dick face.

MORE GRACIELA

I have watched Graciela all her life growing up, and there were things I saw that bothered me. I noticed that she was becoming quite materialistic and selfish. I shouldn't have been surprised. Her mother was always more interested in her girlfriends than her daughter, and didn't give Graciela much attention. Instead giving Graciela attention, Valeria bought things for her. When Graciela started fooling around with a couple of drug dealers, it really worried me. She wasn't just seeing José, who was a few years older, but also had another boyfriend at the same time, Oscar. And Oscar was quite a bit older and a drug dealer, too. He was over thirty years old, and was buying her all kinds of gifts. She was only fourteen when they started, and it was easy to turn her head. I didn't like it one bit, but I wasn't able to do anything about it. Oscar was feared in the neighborhood and I was afraid of him too. If I threatened to punish Graciela, I knew she would just go live with Oscar. I thought that if she was still living with me I might be able to influence her a little. That is what I was hoping.

I always got along well enough with Graciela except when it came to money. She was fine letting me pay for everything and give her a place to stay, but when she came into some money, she would never share. There were times in my life when I didn't have to worry about money, but that was in the past. It is hard for me to just survive, pay rent and buy food. Graciela ate my food, stayed in my place and used electricity and water but never thought about helping me out even when she had some money. We started to fight about that. She said that what was hers was hers. I thought she should help me a little. We would fight about money and she would go away for a few days or longer. She even went back to live with Valeria a few times after Valeria broke up with Liliana, but she always came back to live with me or maybe my mother after a little while.

I don't have a good feeling about Graciela's future. She got herself a false ID card and even asked me if I knew any gringos who would pay her for sex. I didn't want anything to do with that. She was only sixteen at the time. Graciela was going to school until she started seeing Oscar and José, and she didn't have to quit, but she did. Valeria would certainly have kept paying for her studies. But Graciela preferred to hang out with drug dealers rather than go to school. She had advantages I never had, but she seems to be headed for a life a lot like mine. One good thing is that she hasn't gotten pregnant yet. Not yet, thank God.

I might have tolerated her selfishness but she did something I just can't forgive her for. I don't trust Graciela and I needed her to go pick up some mota for me from Oscar. I had a gringo friend who wanted some. But I don't trust Graciela by herself, so I asked Milena to go with her up to Oscar's to make sure nothing funny happened. Well, they went up the street and got the mota and started back to the apartment. On the way back they went into a little pulperia and Milena saw Graciela sending a short text message to somebody, something like "now." They left the pulperia and began to walk home when some guy came out of nowhere and started hitting Milena. Graciela took off running and left Milena to get beaten up.

Milena and I couldn't figure out what happened right away, but the truth came out in a few days. The reason that this guy attacked Milena was because Graciela had sold some drugs for Oscar but had spent the money before paying him. Graciela had told Oscar that Milena stole the drugs so Oscar wouldn't blame Graciela for not having the money or the drugs. Then she set

Milena up to get beaten. Well, that was the final straw! Graciela had been selfish and irresponsible before, but she had never done anything like get somebody beaten up so she could steal. Even my mother threw her out. My mother may forgive her someday but I never will. Graciela has turned into a very bad person and I don't want to have anything to do with her ever again. She's back living with Valeria for now, but who knows how long that will last.

Valeria isn't with Joaquin or Liliana now, she has a new boyfriend, a Nica named Leandro, who she was cheating with while she was with Joaquin. She broke up with Joaquin when she got pregnant again, probably by Leandro. But she miscarried and nobody will ever know whose baby it was. On top of all that, she just got fired from her job managing that fast-food restaurant. Eduardo and Joaquin are still there, but she's gone. Pati told me they caught her stealing, and that was that. I hope her Nica is earning some money. Valeria will probably find another job somewhere; she's a hard worker, really. She's just not as honest as she should be, or not as careful.

What I hear from Pati, Graciela is spending a fair amount of time with Oscar, though I think it's just for what she can get. She jokes about him and calls him "cosita" [little thing] because his penis is small. She's only about seven months from 18 years old, and I'm pretty sure she will be working the bars as a prostitute as soon as she gets her ID to prove she's 18. She's doing sex for money now, but can't go into bars to work. She's pretty and likes sex, so she should do alright until she gets older or gets fat. She could have done other things in her life if she had stayed in school, but a lazy and greedy girl like her doesn't want to work hard for a little money. She's seen quite a lot in her life, and I don't think she's afraid of that kind of life, even though she's heard some of my stories and seen how life is for me.

I still don't think she realizes what the life is really like and how dangerous and ugly it can be. There was a girl who came in the Arenal bar a few times who had a pretty obvious cocaine or crack problem. My friend Teddy went with her one time and she stole his camera. I didn't see her for a few months, then ran into her at El Capitan one night with her mother's boyfriend, an older gringo in his sixties. The gringo was plenty drunk, but the girl, Jessica, was drunk almost to the point of being unconscious. She had also put on a lot of weight, so maybe she had stopped doing crack. But she still didn't want to be sober. Alcohol was her drug of choice now. She was obviously very drunk... dangerously drunk. I remember thinking to myself that something really bad might happen to her, being that drunk.

It was about two months later that my friend Jeni had talked to Jessica's mother, and the mother told Jeni that Jessica had been out one night the week before, and her body was found in the streets, raped and murdered. Jessica was only nineteen, and now she's dead. I can't say I knew her, really, but it hit me hard. I couldn't help thinking about Graciela. This was the life she was choosing.

I hope she doesn't end up like Jessica.

ALSO BY THOMAS RAY O'BRIEN

Dances with Prostitutes – Costa Rica Style

MORE Dances with Prostitutes – Costa Rica Style

Clueless Clyde in Costa Rica
Complete!

Thomas Ray O'Brien

Clueless Clyde – Complete (Volumes 1, 2 and 3)

ABOUT THE AUTHOR:

Thomas Ray O'Brien has lived in San José, Costa Rica since June of 2004. He is a retired musician and computer programmer. He is a native of Northern California and spent much of his life shuffling between the SF Bay area and the Central Valley. Studied psychology and philosophy at UC Berkeley and CSU San José before realizing he was not cut out to be an academic.

To pass the time, he writes, dabbles in photography and video as well as music. Oh and he likes to hang out with prostitutes.

He has sworn off golf, forever, as a public service. He has never been married and has no children, which is also a public service. His blog is http://www.lovecostaricastyle.com

https://www.facebook.com/thomasrayobrien

and

https://www.facebook.com/thomas.obrien.319247

and

https://www.facebook.com/pages/Love-Costa-Rica-Style/100280950064240

Email Thomasrayobrien@gmail.com

On twitter, @thomasreyobrien (notice the "e" in rey)

www.ingramcontent.com/pod-product-compliance
Lightning Source LLC
Chambersburg PA
CBHW060621290526
45793CB00001B/101